Political Correctness

Other Books in the Current Controversies Series

Political Correctness

Rachel Bozek, Book Editor

Published in 2018 by Greenhaven Publishing, LLC
353 3rd Avenue, Suite 255, New York, NY 10010

First Edition

Articles in Greenhaven Publishing anthologies are often edited for length to meet page
requirements. In addition, original titles of these works are changed to clearly present
the main thesis and to explicitly indicate the author's opinion. Every effort is made to
ensure that Greenhaven Publishing accurately reflects the original intent of the authors.
Every effort has been made to trace the owners of the copyrighted material.

Cover image: Stephen Orsillo/Alamy Stock Photo

Library of Congress Cataloging-in-Publication Data

Names: Bozek, Rachel, editor.
Title: Political correctness / edited by Rachel Bozek.
Description: New York : Greenhaven Publishing, 2018. | Series: Current
controversies | Includes bibliographic references and index. | Audience: Grades 9-
12.
Identifiers: LCCN ISBN 9781534500990 (library bound) | ISBN 9781534500976
(pbk.)
Subjects: LCSH: Freedom of expression--United States. | Political correctness—
United States. | Intellectual freedom--United States.
Classification: LCC KF4770.P65 2018 | DDC 323.44'30973--dc23

Manufactured in the United States of America

Website: http://greenhavenpublishing.com

Contents

Chapter 1: Are We Too Easily Offended by Language?

> *Jesse Walker*
> The debate over the meaning and significance of the term "political correctness" is hardly new. As the concept has evolved, it has continued to spark discussion and controversy.

Yes: We Are Too Easily Offended by Language

> *Shaheen Pasha*
> With an entire generation being raised on safe spaces and trigger warnings, how will the press be affected by journalists who cannot handle uncomfortable situations?

> *Asa J*
> The terrifying concept of "thought policing" has evolved from being a literary trope to an actual practice.

No: We Are Not Too Easily Offended by Language

> *Kevin Carson*
> Those who complain about political correctness turning into the Thought Police need to understand why the PC culture evolved in the first place.

> *Peter Kilroy*
> A debate over the terms used in Australia's historical narrative serve as an example of why precision is so important. Pejorative labels

of "politically correct" should not be thrown about lightly when distinctions in rhetoric have important implications to subjugated people.

Chapter 2: Are College Campuses Too Politically Correct?

David A. Tomar

While college students are perceived by many to be oversensitive and even coddled, their environment is also an ideal place for full exercise of the First Amendment.

Yes: College Campuses Are Too Politically Correct

Daniel J. Mitchell

There are many examples of political correctness taken surprisingly far on college campuses around the United States.

Greg Lukianoff

Speech policing has been on the rise over the past two decades, and it is becoming a threat to freedom of speech on college campuses.

No: College Campuses Are Not Too Politically Correct

Jennifer Wallin-Ruschman and Mazna Patka

There is an inherent value to safe spaces on college campuses. They are the ideal settings in which to create social change.

Tony Pollard

Sensitivity, particularly with regard to topics dealing with graphic and potentially traumatic content, enables students to learn in a setting where they feel secure.

Chapter 3: Should Political Correctness Be Applied to Social Media and the News?

Chapter 3: Should Political Correctness Be Applied to Social Media and the News?

Keith Hampton, Lee Rainie, Weixu Lu, Maria Dwyer, Inyoung Shin, and Kristen Purcell

Social media has a direct impact on the way we discuss sensitive issues, but not always in the way we might expect.

Yes: Political Correctness Should Be Applied to Social Media and the News

Lance Selfa

The effort the author refers to as the "Anti-PC Crusade" has had a real—and negative—effect on American culture, in large part by way of the news.

Gene Demby

A study reveals that individuals who establish a comfort level of communication can generate more—and higher level—ideas in collaboration with one another.

No: Political Correctness Should Not Be Applied to Social Media and the News

Luis R. Miranda

Political correctness is nothing but a tool for gaining power for those who feel that they've been victimized by society. Social media is helping it spread like wildfire.

Walter Brasch

All too often, publishers and news media gloss over—or ignore—the truth and instead give the public the most easy-to-swallow or entertaining content available.

Chapter 4: Has PC Culture Gone Too Far?

Foreword

Controversy" is a word that has an undeniably unpleasant connotation. It carries a definite negative charge. Controversy can spoil family gatherings, spread a chill around classroom and campus discussion, inflame public discourse, open raw civic wounds, and lead to the ouster of public officials. We often feel that controversy is almost akin to bad manners, a rude and shocking eruption of that which must not be spoken or thought of in polite, tightly guarded society. To avoid controversy, to quell controversy, is often seen as a public good, a victory for etiquette, perhaps even a moral or ethical imperative.

Yet the studious, deliberate avoidance of controversy is also a whitewashing, a denial, a death threat to democracy. It is a false sterilizing, sanitizing, and superficial ordering of the messy, ragged, chaotic, and at times ugly processes by which a healthy democracy identifies and confronts challenges, engages in passionate debate about appropriate approaches and solutions, and arrives at something like a consensus and a broadly accepted and supported way forward. Controversy is the megaphone, the speaker's corner, the public square through which the citizenry finds and uses its voice. Controversy is the life's blood of our democracy and absolutely essential to the vibrant health of our society.

Our present age is certainly no stranger to controversy. We are consumed by fierce debates about technology, privacy, political correctness, poverty, violence, crime and policing, guns, immigration, civil and human rights, terrorism, militarism, environmental protection, and gender and racial equality. Loudly competing voices are raised every day, shouting opposing opinions, putting forth competing agendas, and summoning starkly different visions of a utopian or dystopian future. Often these voices attempt to shout the others down; there is precious little listening and considering in the cacophonous din. Yet listening and considering, too, are essential to the health of a democracy. If controversy is democracy's lusty lifeblood, respectful listening and careful thought are its higher faculties, its brain, its conscience.

Current Controversies does not shy away from or attempt to hush the loudly competing voices. It seeks to provide readers with as wide and representative as possible a range of articulate voices on any given controversy of the day. It separates each voice out to allow it to be heard clearly and fairly, and encourages careful listening to each of these well-crafted, thoughtfully expressed opinions, supplied by some of today's leading academics, thinkers, analysts, politicians, policy makers, economists, activists, change agents, and advocates. Only after listening to a wide range of opinions on an issue, evaluating the strengths and weaknesses of each argument, assessing how well the facts and available evidence mesh with the stated opinions and conclusions, and thoughtfully and critically examining one's own beliefs and conscience can the reader begin to arrive at his or her own conclusions and articulate his or her own stance on the spotlighted controversy.

This process is facilitated and supported in each Current Controversies volume by an introduction and chapter overviews that provide readers with the essential context they need to begin engaging with the spotlighted controversies, with the debates surrounding them, and with their own perhaps shifting or nascent opinions on them. Chapters are organized around several key questions that are answered with diverse opinions representing all points on the political spectrum. In its content, organization, and methodology, readers are encouraged to determine the authors' point of view and purpose, interrogate and analyze the various arguments and their rhetoric and structure, evaluate the arguments' strengths and weaknesses, test their claims against available facts and evidence, judge the validity of the reasoning, and bring into clearer, sharper focus the reader's own beliefs and conclusions and how they may differ from or align with those in the collection or those of classmates.

Research has shown that reading comprehension skills improve dramatically when students are provided with compelling, intriguing, and relevant "discussable" texts. The subject matter of these collections could not be more compelling, intriguing, or urgently relevant to today's students and the world they are poised to inherit. The anthologized articles also provide the basis for stimulating, lively, and passionate classroom debates. Students who are compelled to anticipate objections to their own argument and identify the flaws in those of an opponent read more carefully, think more critically, and steep themselves in relevant context, facts, and information more thoroughly. In short, using discussable text of the kind provided by every single volume in the Current Controversies series encourages close reading, facilitates reading comprehension, fosters research, strengthens critical thinking, and greatly enlivens and energizes classroom discussion and participation. The entire learning process is deepened, extended, and strengthened.

If we are to foster a knowledgeable, responsible, active, and engaged citizenry, we must provide readers with the intellectual, interpretive, and critical-thinking tools and experience necessary to make sense of the world around them and of the all important debates and arguments that inform it. We must encourage them not to run away from or attempt to quell controversy but to embrace it in a responsible, conscientious, and thoughtful way, to sharpen and strengthen their own informed opinions by listening to and critically analyzing those of others. This series encourages respectful engagement with and analysis of current controversies and competing opinions and fosters a resulting increase in the strength and rigor of one's own opinions and stances. As such, it helps readers assume their rightful place in the public square and provides them with the skills necessary to uphold their awesome responsibility—guaranteeing the continued and future health of a vital, vibrant, and free democracy.

Introduction

"Political Correctness is now, more than ever, a commanding force on our society."

"... like most decisions a college must make, political correctness is an economic one."

"... political correctness is today most commonly bandied as an insult ..."

"Political correctness is a concept brandished with so much hostility that incidents suggesting its impracticality are trumpeted as evidence that free speech is dead."

A s evidenced by the above quotations, political correctness can mean many things to many people. The concept of being politically correct (PC) is not a new one, and over the years, it has enjoyed an on-again, off-again presence in the public consciousness. As Jesse Walker explains in chapter 1, "People have been putting the words 'politically' and 'correct' together in various contexts for ages."

In recent years, however, the concept has been turned completely "on" again and is certainly more of a clear-cut, right-versus-left issue than ever before. By the time November 2016 rolled around, the PC debate had become one of the cornerstones of the US presidential election, and the topic reached a new height in terms of its own ubiquity. As Aoife Kelly mentions in chapter 4, "This current strain of anti-PC activism seems to be stronger than any previous manifestations."

Individuals—and groups, for that matter—who see political correctness as a problem generally agree with one another that "believers" are too easily offended and that "PC culture" currently plays too big a role in our everyday lives. Some liken political correctness to censorship, even calling advocates the "thought police."

However, those who are referred to as PC don't see it this way. These individuals and groups are, more often than not, liberal and generally share the point of view that language should reflect mindfulness and inclusiveness. From their perspective, political correctness is not a form of censorship but rather the proper way to express oneself in the modern pluralistic culture.

While it was around for quite a while beforehand, the term "politically correct" became part of our vernacular in the 1990s. Since then the "anti-PC" camp has held the belief that individuals— or organizations, including private companies—can't say anything anymore without offending someone, and they find this to be frustrating and unnecessary. Critics of political correctness argue that the PC culture is actually a form of censorship.

On the flip side, those who believe in political correctness hold fast that PC is not a form of censorship but rather the proper way to express oneself in modern culture. The debate over the offensiveness of many sports team names, for example, is nothing new and continues to make headlines every so often.

On a micro level, college campuses have become prime settings for debates over political correctness. Are college administrations— and students, for that matter—too concerned with political correctness? Are trigger warnings necessary or overkill? Isn't the college a safe enough space already, without having to designate itself as a safe space? Some say yes to all of the above. Others would answer with a resounding "absolutely not!"

Some argue that the concern over safe spaces and trigger warnings is unnecessary and that language on campuses is influenced more than it should be by concerns about political correctness. However, the flip side of this viewpoint is that the college setting is the ideal context within which young adults can—and should—learn to be measured, considerate, and inclusive. They are in an ideal place to give political correctness real consideration and incorporate it into their everyday lives and language.

The question of just how much political correctness should be applied on social media and in the news is another topic of great debate. From TV news to magazines and newspapers to, of course, Facebook and other social media platforms, maintaining a sense of awareness and sensitivity while creating—and responding to—content can go a long way. However, some argue that this is where the First Amendment's efficacy is most clearly tested, as they don't want to "water down" their language.

With all of this in mind, the question of "How far is too far when it comes to PC culture?" is quite relevant. Conservative writers, politicians, and other right-leaning public figures believe PC culture has already reached an unnecessary extreme. However, the sentiment that PC culture is an important element of how information is processed and distributed remains strong as well. Read on to get a taste of the debate in *Current Controversies: Political Correctness,* and see where your own viewpoint falls.

Chapter 1

Are We Too Easily Offended by Language?

Overview: Perceptions of the Meaning of "Politically Correct" Have Evolved Over Several Decades

Jesse Walker

Jesse Walker is books editor of Reason *magazine. He is the author of several books, including* Rebels on the Air: An Alternative History of Radio in America *and* The United States of Paranoia: A Conspiracy Theory.

Amanda Taub's Vox piece denying the existence of political correctness does get one thing right: The phrase political correctness "has no actual fixed or specific meaning." What it does have, though Taub doesn't explore this, is a history of meanings: a series of ways different people have deployed the term, often for radically different purposes. Unpack that history, and you can unpack a lot of the debates going on today.

People have been putting the words "politically" and "correct" together in various contexts for ages, but for our purposes the story begins in the middle of the 20th century, as various Marxist-Leninist sects developed a distinctive cant. One of the terms they liked to use was "politically correct," as in "What is needed now is a politically correct, class-conscious and militant leadership, which will lead an armed struggle to abolish the whole system of exploitation of man by man in Indonesia and establish a workers state!" It was a phrase for the sort of radical who was deeply interested in establishing and enforcing the "correct line," to borrow another term of the day. If you were the sort of radical who was *not* interested in establishing and enforcing the correct line, you were bound to start mocking this way of talking, and by the end of the '60s the mockers were flinging the phrase back at the drones. In 1969, for example, when Dana Beal of the White

"What the Hell Does 'Politically Correct' Mean?: A Short History," by Jesse Walker, January 30, 2015. Reprinted by permission.

Panther Party defended the counterculture against its critics on the straight left, he argued that freely experimenting was more important than trying "to be perfectly politically 'correct.'" A year later, in the seminal feminist anthology *Sisterhood is Powerful*, Robin Morgan derided male editors who had "the best intentions of being politically 'correct'" but couldn't resist butting in with their own ideas. In the new usage, which soon superceded the old Leninist lingo pretty much entirely, "politically correct" was an unkind term for leftists who acted as though good politics were simply a matter of mastering the right jargon.

Meanwhile, a similar but slightly different approach to the phrase emerged. In '80s issues of magazines like *Mother Jones* or *Ms.*, "politically correct" could describe a consumer good or a lifestyle choice. The tone here was usually lightly self-mocking, as you'd expect when words once associated with a shifting Maoist party line were now being applied to an exercise book or a fake fur. But some people did use it earnestly, perhaps because they weren't in on the joke, perhaps because they just thought the term was too good to go to waste. In the early '90s, a woman told me that she and her friends had often said "politically correct" without any irony when she was an undergraduate at Bryn Mawr. She wasn't happy when she started hearing people use the expression disdainfully.

[...]

By then the term was fairly well-established on American campuses. When future Clinton speechwriter Jeff Shesol debuted his comic strip *Thatch* in Brown's student newspaper in 1988, he included a faux superhero called Politically Correct Person, a character forever correcting people's language and consumer choices. The phrase persisted in the more radical segments of the left as well. When I was attending the University of Michigan, one of my colleagues at the student radio station edited a queer/punk zine called *P.C. Casualties*, which ran this righteous rant in 1991: "As if *bullying* prank phone calls from those young Republican [expletive] weren't enough, now we have half-assed, pseudo-radical academics playing the same old power games as well. Yeah, you've got all the 'correct' answers, and even a little power in your corner of this political ghetto. But you're all fake. …All you've managed to do is torture and maim those you really ought to be caring for—your own brothers and sisters. The bodies of P.C. Casualties lay strewn all over, ghosts of dreams too afraid to materialize, and whispers too fearful to make a sound."

That piece was published near the end of the 1990-91 academic year, which also happened to be the year the phrase had its national coming-out party. The December 24, 1990, *Newsweek* featured the words "THOUGHT POLICE" on its cover; inside, a Jerry Adler article argued that "where the PC reigns, one defies it at one's peril." A month later, John Taylor's cover story "Are You Politically Correct?" appeared in *New York* magazine. The *Wall Street Journal* ran a series of pieces attacking political correctness. And around the same time that issue of *P.C. Casualties* appeared, President George Herbert Walker Bush warned the graduating class at Michigan that "the notion of political correctness" was replacing "old prejudices with new ones."

"Politically correct" had now entered the mainstream lexicon—and, maybe more important, the conservative lexicon. But what did people mean when they said it? When that jeremiad in *P.C. Casualties* got down to specifics, it invoked "women banned from the Michigan Womyn's Music Festival for practicing S&M." You weren't likely to see *that* mentioned in a George Will column. So what were the conservatives upset about?

To a large extent, it was the same things critics on the left had been upset about. But there were other complaints here, too. While *Newsweek*'s cover story included anecdotes about censorship and other heavy-handed attempts to impose an orthodoxy, it also veered off periodically into discussions of deconstruction, the Great Books canon, and other subjects that didn't have much to do with civil liberties. Taylor's *New York* story went even further in that direction, including a whole section on Afrocentrism. From 1990 onward, a bunch of longstanding conservative complaints about campus life, particularly its arguments about what was taught in the English departments, were framed as debates about political correctness.

For some on the right, "P.C." began to be a vague way to refer to anything left of center. "*Un*-P.C.," meanwhile, became a phrase people used to pat themselves on the back, not just on the right but in the culture at large. By proclaiming yourself politically incorrect, you were announcing that you were a brave opponent of stultifying orthodoxies, even if your actual opinions were as vanilla as the Michigan Womyn's Music Festival.

On the left, some people embraced the term defensively (at Michigan, several student groups opened the 1991-92 school year by adopting the slogan "PC and Proud"), while others foreshadowed Taub by declaring political correctness a myth. More recently, it's become common to claim that what conservatives call political correctness is really "just politeness." (And indeed, if someone uneducated in the jargon of the week unwittingly uses the wrong language, he may receive the same reaction he'd get at a society dinner for using the wrong fork. But I don't think that's what they mean.)

So maybe Taub's right; maybe we should drop the phrase from our lexicon. Not because it doesn't describe anything, but because it describes so many things that you can't use it without worrying that people won't understand what you're talking about. But I won't scold you if you use it anyway. I wouldn't want to come across as politically correct.

Political Correctness Impedes the Rights of the Press

Shaheen Pasha

Shaheen Pasha is a journalist and assistant professor of international journalism at the University of Massachusetts-Amherst. She has a master's degree in journalism from Columbia Graduate School of Journalism and a bachelor's degree in speech communication from Pace University.

I was in college the first time I heard someone use the N-word. Really use it to describe a group of people. Hip-hop group KRS One was scheduled to play a concert at my ethnically diverse New York City-based university, and I had just excitedly bought my tickets. I sat in the cafeteria with a study group when a white classmate looked over at the poster hanging on the window and laughed, saying it was going to be the night for the n*****s to come out of the jungle and play.

I was stunned. I looked around at my group and realized that I was the only one of color at the table. And no one else batted an eyelash.

College was also where I got into a yelling match with a friend during a Middle Eastern history class over a Muslim woman's right to wear hijab. It was where I heard loud, violent-sounding sex from a dorm room on my floor, where I learned of a suicide attempt by another student, and where I was stalked by a classmate, who would sneak into the residence hall and wait for me in the communal lounge.

"The Fallacy of 'Safe Space' on College Campuses," by Shaheen Pasha, MediaShift, December 2, 2015. Reprinted by permission.

No Safe Space

College is not a safe space. It was never intended to be. It is a place where debates can turn heated and ugly and the cruel realities of the world come crashing down on students, preparing them for the very real discourse they will face upon graduation. It is a time to grow out of the protective cocoon of childhood and face the fact that the world can be an unpleasant place.

But a recent trend on college campuses is threatening to shut down that natural maturation process in the quest to create a "safe space" for students. Recent University of Missouri protests against the lack of action against racism on campus took a notable turn after protestors and faculty attempted to bar reporters from entering a public place they had claimed as a safe space. One of the motivations for the media ban was that student protestors were afraid that the media would warp their narrative.

That concept took on an even more insidious twist when Smith College and Amherst College—two of the most liberal and open-minded universities in the country—organized sit-in protests in solidarity with the University of Missouri. But this exercise in liberalism and free speech took a decidedly anti-liberal tone. Amherst College activists issued a series of demands that included punishing counter-protestors with a racial re-education program and potential disciplinary action. In essence, only some views should be allowed on campus because other views apparently make people uncomfortable.

Smith College protestors took it a step further and banned media from covering their event unless the journalists came out in public support of their cause. Otherwise, they wanted a safe space free of journalists who may distort their message and cause emotional distress to the protestors.

Let that sink in.

The United States Constitution allows for the right to assembly. It allows passionate college students the freedom of speech to raise their voices against authority figures, whether a university chancellor or the president of the United States. And students can do that without fear of retribution. But the Constitution also allows for the freedom of press in which reporters can freely cover public demonstrations. It allows journalists to have the same freedom of speech that the protestors have. Somehow those freedoms have fallen to the wayside on college campuses today.

Representations And Rights

The argument raised by protestors is that the media can manipulate and misrepresent the facts to create an untrue picture. I'm not debating that. I understand the concern. I am a person of color and a Muslim. That's a double whammy when it comes to representation in the media. But before becoming an assistant professor of journalism, I was a full-time journalist for 15 years. I traveled the globe and have seen first-hand how the same story can be shifted to fit corporate agendas and personal biases. I have seen how reporters of color can be steamrolled in a newsroom. I teach my journalism students about it in class. I warn against the dangers of it and how they can fight it. But I also recognize that the rights of the press have to be protected.

The student protestors' insistence on attempting to control their message and the way it is presented is actually taking away from the credibility of their cause. You cannot criticize a university or society for stomping on the rights of the people in one breath while trampling on the rights of the media—the watchdog of the people—in the next. It also shows an astonishing naivete on the part of the protest organizers that threaten to overshadow and undermine the very real and justified grievances that they have. No journalist, trained in the ethics of the profession and with a sense of personal integrity, should agree to support any cause in order to report on it. Those who do need to come to my introduction to journalism class for a reality check on the profession.

As a professor, I am sensitive to the needs of my students, but I cannot coddle them. I have had students walk out of a class when I taught about the horrific 2012 Delhi rape without offering a trigger warning. Another former student came to my office to demand an apology for showing an Al Jazeera report on the families of the Dimona suicide bombers in Israel because "terrorists do not deserve to have stories done about them that may humanize them in any way." And I've had former students angered by class discussions on Ferguson and race relations in the country that offended them as white people.

Impeding journalism in the quest for safe spaces is a no-win situation. As a journalism instructor, I will be sending out the next generation of reporters to witness and report on the horrors of the world. If they cannot handle the stress of an uncomfortable class discussion, they will have a hard time in the profession. And as a college professor, I deeply respect and admire the convictions of the impassioned student activists on campus who want to create a better world. I salute you and support you. But once the activism impedes on the rights of others and forces them to share your beliefs, well-intentioned liberalism can take on an ugly shade of authoritarianism. That I can't support.

Political Correctness Is Encouraging a "Thought Police"

Asa J

Asa J is the handle of a conservative writer and a frequent contributor to Copblock.org.

The term "thought police" was popularized by George Orwell in his 1949 dystopian novel, *Nineteen Eighty-Four*. In the book, Orwell's Thought Police are charged with uncovering and punishing "thought-crime" and thought-criminals throughout the fictional superstate of Oceania.

The secret police agency uses propaganda, psychological methods, and omnipresent surveillance to search, find, monitor, and arrest members of society who could potentially challenge the authority of "Big Brother."

Likewise, all across the western world, individuals are currently being jailed and prosecuted for expressing legitimate political views deemed "hateful" or "extreme" by governments.

Recent examples include a U.K. politician being arrested and charged last year under section 4 of the country's Public Order Act of 1986—which defines "racially aggravated public order offenses," as "abusive or insulting words or behavior"—for reciting a Winston Churchill quote critical of Islam.

In places like Sweden and Canada, Christian pastors have been arrested and even sentenced to prison for espousing biblical positions on homosexuality. Across Europe, questioning the official version of Holocaust will get you locked up.

Even in the United States, a similar style of thought-policing has steadily infiltrated the culture over the past several decades, culminating with the Obama Administrations unveiling of a new

"Political Correctness Means a Draconian Police State," ASA J, Cop Block, October 17, 2015. http://www.copblock.org/143976/political-correctness-means-draconian-police-state/. Licensed under CC BY-SA 2.0.

global police force which is to be utilized to "fight extremism" in major cities across the country.

At the end of last month, Attorney General Loretta Lynch announced at the United Nations that her office would be working in several American cities to integrate what has been dubbed the "Strong Cities Network" (SCN) in a move toward international consolidation of law-enforcement agencies around the globe.

Called the "Launch of Strong Cities Network to Strengthen Community Resilience Against Violent Extremism," the international program already includes 23 cities around the world including New York, Atlanta, Denver, and Minneapolis in the United States.

Decried by critics as amounting to "nothing less than the overriding of American laws, up to and including the United States Constitution, in favor of United Nations laws" that would inevitably be implemented in the country without any Congressional oversight, the Obama Department of Justice described the program in a press release stating:

> Cities are vital partners in international efforts to build social cohesion and resilience to violent extremism. Local communities and authorities are the most credible and persuasive voices to challenge violent extremism in all of its forms and manifestations in their local contexts. While many cities and local authorities are developing innovative responses to address this challenge, no systematic efforts are in place to share experiences, pool resources and build a community of cities to inspire local action on a global scale.
>
> The SCN will connect cities, city-level practitioners and the communities they represent through a series of workshops, trainings and sustained city partnerships. Network participants will also contribute to and benefit from an online repository of municipal-level good practices and web-based training modules and will be eligible for grants supporting innovative, local initiatives and strategies that will contribute to building social cohesion and resilience to violent extremism.

The SCN will include an International Steering Committee of approximately 25 cities and other sub-national entities from different regions that will provide the SCN with its strategic direction. The SCN will also convene an International Advisory Board, which includes representatives from relevant city-focused networks, to help ensure SCN builds upon their work.

New York Mayor Bill de Blasio has already lauded the program and its intent to protect citizens against "all forms of violent extremism, whether it's based in religious, or racial, or nationalistic, or ideological intolerance." (sic)

Its important to understand that the United States government has made it clear over and over again—they perceive American enemies to be gun owners and libertarians.

One of the most egregious confirmations of this was back in 2012 when a report published by The National Consortium for the Study of Terrorism and Responses to Terrorism (START) stated that Americans "reverent of individual liberty" and others adamant about protecting their personal freedoms, are "extreme right-wing terrorists."

In that paper, Hot Spots of Terrorism and Other Crimes in the United States, 1970-2008, researchers used definitions from another START study, 2011's Profiles of Perpetrators of Terrorism, to characterize what traits should be considered when describing right-wing terrorists.

Those definitions include:

- Americans who believe their "way of life" is under attack
- Americans who are "fiercely nationalistic (as opposed to universal and international in orientation)"
- People who consider themselves "anti-global" (presumably those who are wary of the loss of American sovereignty)
- Americans who are "suspicious of centralized federal authority"
- People who are "opposed to abortion and support the second Amendment"
- Americans who are "reverent of individual liberty"

- People who "believe in conspiracy theories that involve grave threat to national sovereignty and/or personal liberty."

START—a University of Maryland project funded directly by the Department of Homeland Security, released a report last year which collected information from state and local fusion centers, the FBI's Joint Terrorism Task Force, the DHS, BATF, DEA, ICE, and state and local homeland security and anti-terrorism task forces.

The report found that the so-called "Sovereign Citizen Movement" has been named the number one domestic terrorist threat in America, with "52 percent of respondents agree[ing] and 34 percent strongly agree[ing] that sovereign citizens constitute the most serious terrorist threat"—opposed to 39 percent of respondents who agreed and 28 percent who strongly agreed that Islamic extremists are the most serious threat.

Self-described sovereign citizens take the position that they are answerable only to common law and are not subject to any statutes or proceedings at the federal, state, or municipal levels. They especially reject most forms of taxation as illegitimate. Participants in the movement argue the concept is in opposition to "federal citizens" who, they say, have unknowingly forfeited their rights by accepting some aspect of federal law.

"The 2013-14 study results show that law enforcement's top concern is sovereign citizens," the START report states. "Although Islamic extremists remain a major concern for law enforcement, they are no longer their top concern."

The report recommends state and federal law enforcement share intelligence data on targeted groups, develop "tactical responses" to threats and "act on that information to prevent or mitigate threats." Among the threat groups listed include Militia members, tax-protesters, and Christian Idenitarians.

Federal authorities, particularly the Department of Homeland Security, during both the Obama and Bush administrations, have been involved in producing a plethora of literature portraying liberty lovers and limited-government advocates as terrorists.

One of the most blatant examples was the infamous 2009 MIAC report, published by the Missouri Information Analysis Center which framed Ron Paul supporters, libertarians, people who display bumper stickers, people who own gold, or even people who fly a U.S. flag, as potential terrorists.

Even everyday behaviors are now regarded as suspicious by the United States government. Under the FBI's Communities Against Terrorism program, the bulk purchase of food, using cash to pay for a cup of coffee, and showing an interest in web privacy when using the Internet in a public place are all labeled as a potential indication of terrorist activity.

The agenda to consolidate federal authority over local law enforcement was typified best in a white paper presented to the House Permanent Select Committee on Intelligence in 2012— which outlined an "evolving mission" for Homeland Security that moves away from fighting terrorism and towards growing a vast domestic intelligence network that would expand integration with local and state agencies and private-public partnerships already underway via regional fusion centers.

Crafted by the Aspen Institute Homeland Security Group, co-chaired by former DHS chief Michael Chertoff, the report proposed a transition from outwardly dealing with the threats posed by terrorism towards intelligence gathering "focused on more specific homeward-focused areas."

DHS maintains that "the threat grows more localized" which requires the militarization of local police in major cities and the training of staff from local agencies to make sure that oversight is restricted to the federal government.

The creation and implementation of fusion centers in urban areas was to "serve as focal points within the state and local environment for the receipt, analysis, gathering, and sharing of threat-related information between the federal government and state, local, tribal, territorial (SLTT) and private sector partners."

"As the threat grows more localized," the report reads, "the federal government's need to train, and even staff, local agencies, such as major city police departments, will grow."

Apparently the need for international involvement in local policing is growing too. According to Attorney General Lynch, the Strong Cities Network scheme "will be run by the Institute for Strategic Dialogue (ISD)"—a left-wing European think-tank.

Knowing that according to the United States governments own reports and documents, liberty-lovers are considered "terrorists," it is important to note that the UN and ISD have similar views and routinely support gun control and other draconian social and speech policies across Europe.

According to an ISD report entitled Old Threat, New Approach: Tackling the Far Right Across Europe, "The project will develop an online tool to provide practical training for practitioners, and will seed a long-term network of experts and practitioners working to counter far-right extremism"—which the group identifies with nationalism, opposition to immigration, and firearm ownership.

President Obama told the UN last week that the U.S. will use "all of our tools" to fight Islamic State terrorists but it's clear from the ISD website what kind of "extremism" it plans on fighting.

Gracing the site are numerous mentions of "far-right extremism across Europe," the increasing legitimization of "anti-immigration and anti-Islamic discourses," "the extreme right," "Islamophobia and anti-immigration sentiment," and "violent right-wing extremism."

In other words, what most Americans consider to be traditional Western values will now be policed as thought-crimes and "terrorism" by international bodies in cities across the country with absolutely no oversight by United States citizens.

Perhaps even more troubling, was a Department of Justice announcement made Wednesday that affirmed that under the umbrella of "Homeland Security," the agency will now be moving away from combating Islamic extremism to fighting home-grown "anti-government groups" with a new "Domestic Terrorism Counsel."

Speaking at a forum hosted by George Washington University's "Program on Extremism," Assistant Attorney General for National Security John Carlin said, "while addressing the evolving international threat of violent extremism, we cannot lose sight of… home-grown violent extremism that can be motivated by… anti-government views, racism, bigotry and anarchy, and other despicable beliefs."

According to Carlin, the domestic terrorism counsel will now assist federal prosecutors nationwide who are working on domestic terrorism cases. He says the counsel will "help shape our strategy and analyze legal gaps or enhancements required to ensure we can combat these threats."

"What causes some confusion is that 'domestic terrorism' is not an offense or a charge," Carlin said. Therefore, domestic terror groups or actors must be prosecuted with firearms or explosives offenses, hate crimes or murder."

The overt unveiling of the thought police in the United States highlights the success of Cultural Marxism in the country. By the end of WWI, socialists realized that the world's proletariat had not heeded Marx's call to rise up in opposition to evil capitalism and to embrace communism instead. Therefore, a new strategy was needed.

Separately, two Marxist theorists, Antonio Gramsci, Founder of the Communist Party of Italy and Georg Lukacs of Hungary, concluded that the Christianized cultural institutions of the West were the obstacle standing in the way of a communist world order.

Gramsci posited that because Christianity had been dominant in the West for over 2000 years, not only was it fused with Western civilization, but it had also corrupted the working class. The West would have to be "de-Christianized," said Gramsci, by the means of what a latter acolyte would call, a "long march through the institutions."

Gramsci had reasoned that the new battleground must become the culture, starting with the traditional family and completely engulfing churches, schools, media, entertainment, civic organizations, literature, science, art, and history. All of these things must be radically transformed as must the social and cultural order if socialism was to be successful.

Additionally, a new socialist movement was to be created through identity politics. In his Prison Notebooks, Gramsci suggested that this new proletariat be comprised of many criminals, women, and racial minorities.

In short, Marxism needed to be translated from economic into cultural terms. Traditional Marxism views the world through the lens of economic determinism. That is to say, there are the oppressed: the workers, and the oppressors: the bourgeoisie and capital owners

Cultural Marxism offered a new class analysis and system of victimology. The oppressed are now: well, everyone that isn't a heterosexual white male, and the oppressors are: white males.

Gramsci's prescription, along with Lukacs' insights gleamed from implementing similar operations as Deputy Commissar for Culture in the short-lived Bolshevik Era Bela Kun regime in Hungary—established the precursor to what was known as the Frankfurt School in Weimar Germany. Among its founders were Lukacs, Herbert Marcuse, and Theodor Adorno.

The school was a multidisciplinary effort which included sociologists, sexologists, and psychologists seeking to synthesize the works of thinkers like Hegel, Marx, Kant, Weber and Freud into an all encompassing "critical" social theory that principally employed the Hegelian dialectical method with its emphasis on dialectic and contradiction as inherent properties of human reality.

With the rise of Hitler in the 1930s, many Frankfurt school intellectuals moved to America, taking up positions in key U.S. universities, and the rest is history.

Building on the earlier Fabian Society strategy of "gradualism," as opposed to an outright revolutionary transition to socialism, the Cultural Marxists initiated the slow infiltration, subversion, and usurpation of traditional American cultural institutions like academia, silencing all dissenters of their agenda as hateful bigots, racists, and homophobes.

When examining the microcosm of political correctness on college campuses, its totalitarian nature becomes clear. Universities have become nothing more than mini-North-Koreas with their own internal legal systems that ruin the lives of anyone who dares to speak out against the Cultural Marxist indoctrination or selective privilege given to so-called "victim groups" by administrators and professors under the auspices of "social justice."

This paradigm has been slowly transitioning from institutions of higher learning to the rest of the society at large. With the announcement of a new global police force and domestic terrorism counsel to fight "extremism," political correctness will invariably come to define the modern American state, as it has done in many other Western countries where free-speech no longer exists.

Thoughtful Language Is Essential for a Culture of Inclusiveness

Kevin Carson

Kevin Carson is a senior fellow of the Center for a Stateless Society and holds the center's Karl Hess Chair in Social Theory. His work includes Studies in Mutualist Political Economy, Organization Theory: A Libertarian Perspective, *and* The Homebrew Industrial Revolution: A Low-Overhead Manifesto. *He also writes at his blog,* The Mutualist Blog.

In all the damage assessments and recriminations following the presidential election, one theme I've seen way too much of is blaming Trump's victory on "political correctness." One person blamed the Left for "demonizing white men" for the past eight years instead of focusing on economic and class issues. Another clutched his pearls about what a dumb strategic move it was to dismiss most of Trump's supporters as "deplorables." And at Reason, human dumpster fire Robby Soave— whose shtik seems to be retyping old Reed Irvine and Dinesh D'Souza screeds with his name on them—literally lays the blame for Trump at the feet of campus speech codes, trigger warnings and safe spaces. (No, if anything defeated Clinton it was stay-at-home Democratic voters disgusted by a Democratic Party that embraced way too many of the same neoliberal—not genuinely libertarian—economic policies favored by Reason.)

Everywhere we see the atmosphere of grievance. Racists, sexists, xenophobes and homophobes, they say, are right to feel affronted at attacks on their bigotry. And even if the criticism is valid, marginalized people should still have tried to be less confrontational in order to avoid alienating all the working class white people whose support we needed to defeat fascism. For

"No, 'Identity Politics' Didn't Elect Trump," Kevin Carson, The Center for a Stateless Society, November 14, 2016.

real: a Greek anarchist literally asked me last spring if standing up for principle on gay rights was worth the increased risk of losing an election to a fascist. Freddie DeBoer is pushing this line of crap now, although he uses weasel words like "liberals with academic vocabularies" because he won't come right out and say black and LGBT people should be quiet so working class whites won't be offended.

But the cultural Right's sense of grievance is utter nonsense. For people who complain so much about the "politics of victimhood," they play the victim card better than anybody else.

Long ago, as a child, I can remember hearing old folks complain that "this country's been going to pot ever since all these people started screaming about their 'rights.'" And that's still the attitude of those who talk about "taking our country back."

Whatever they think of marginalized people demanding their rights, they sure aren't modest about the rights they claim for themselves. They think they have the right to decide what languages people speak, what religious garb they wear, who they marry, and what bathrooms they go to. And when they talk about PC as an assault on their freedom, what they're referring to is their freedom to prohibit other people from doing things they disapprove of. You can't even say "Happy Holidays" to them without them whining about a "War on Christmas." For all their mockery of "safe spaces" and "trigger warnings," they're the most emotionally fragile and easily offended people in existence.

They actually talk about "Thought Police," and sidle up to other white males with "I guess we're not allowed to say this any more, but …"

If you compare their complaints to the complaints of the marginalized people they criticize, they're completely asymmetrical. Women in hijabs have to worry about being verbally and physically assaulted when they leave their homes. Unarmed black people have to worry about being shot in the back and having drop guns planted on their bodies, or being killed in "nickel rides" by sadistic cops. Gay and trans people have to worry about being stomped to death.

So if you think you're living in a totalitarian nightmare because you have to worry about somebody giving you a dirty look for saying the n-word, or because you're expected not to throw a tantrum when you see a woman in a hijab or two men kissing, I've got the world's smallest violin. And if you think that's a sufficient grievance to justify voting for a crypto-fascist just to "teach 'em a lesson," then yes, you are deplorable.

On top of all this, treating the concerns of marginalized people as secondary for the sake of anti-fascist unity is really stupid from a purely strategic point of view. The fight for basic human rights for justice by people of color, women, LGBT people and immigrants isn't a ruling class strategy to divide the producing classes. Rosa Parks didn't refuse to give up her seat, the people at Stonewall didn't decide to stand up and fight, because they'd been paid by elites to do so. But racism, sexism and homophobia themselves really are ruling class weapons to divide us against each other. It isn't marginalized people fighting for their dignity, their very existence, who are being "divisive" and playing into the hands of the capitalist ruling class. The divisive ones, the dupes of the ruling class, are the people who would vote for a fascist just out of spite for having to coexist with people they disapprove of.

Besides, throwing simply marginalized people under the bus by de-prioritizing their issues won't appease the bigots. They won't be satisfied by anything but our active collaboration in oppressing them. So long as they know people they disapprove of even exist, they'll feel victimized by the fact. As my Twitter friend @lbourgie says:

> Over the years there have been several studies and polls that show skewed perception of majorities toward minorities .... Women speaking 15% and being perceived as talking equally as much. Male hiring managers falsely thinking they employ an equal number of women. People in the US and Europe believing there are exponentially more Muslims and people of Middle Eastern descent in their countries. Straight people who think they're being bombarded with gay propaganda if 2%

Political Correctness

of people on TV are LGBT. Christians who sincerely believe they're unfairly penalized and the most disadvantaged group in the US. Knowing all this, why would you embrace a gut emotional reaction that minority group politics—"ID politics"—has drowned out real issues?

That Niemoller poem—"first they came for the socialists…"—isn't just a cliche. When you throw marginalized people under the bus, they won't be there when you need them. That's the significance of the Wobbly slogan "an injury to one is an injury to all."

Abandoning marginalized people is also strategically stupid because it was marginalized people themselves, alienated by Clinton's neoliberalism, who were some of the most likely voters to stay home and vote third party. A lot of ardent Clinton supporters liked to frame the left-wing opposition to HRC as "privileged white males." But the people doing this framing were themselves disproportionately the upper-middle-class white professional types who are the demographic core of establishment liberalism. To the extent that they adhered to any kind of racial or gender politics, it was the outmoded 1970s model of one-dimensional "identity politics" that focused exclusively on putting women and People of Color into the existing power structures, and ignoring class issues, rather than dismantling the power structures themselves.

This ideology is almost the direct opposite of the intersectional politics adhered to by the so-called "SJWs" the cultural Right hates. The left-wing opposition to Clinton is full of People of Color, women, LGBT people (including transgender women excluded by so many second-wave feminists), sex workers, and destitute people from the working poor. Clinton's biggest upper-middle class liberal worshippers—Amanda Marcotte, Peter Daou, Sady Doyle, Clara Jeffery and their ilk—were likely to insult or block such marginalized critics on social media, and continue to insist that they didn't exist, that only right-wingers and "Berniebros" had a problem with Hillary.

African-American voter turnout was actually quite depressed compared to 2012—perhaps because they just couldn't get very

| 38

enthusiastic about a candidate who endorsed her husband's crime bill and welfare "reform" and talked about "super-predators," and whose campaign put out all kinds of racist dog-whistles about Obama in 2008.

And Trump's victory hardly reflects a surge of white racism in response to "political correctness run amok." Trump got two million fewer voters than Romney in 2012. Clinton was rejected because she pursued an economic and foreign policy two microns to the left of the Republican mainstream, and nobody wanted to stand in line 90 minutes for a garbage candidate like her. Period.

So don't blame marginalized people for Clinton.

The society we're aiming for—that we should be aiming for, anyway—is one in which human beings are treated as ends in themselves, and not as means to an end. As the saying goes, the means are the end in progress. You don't build a free and just society by treating some people as more expendable than others.

Language Regarding Subjugated People Has Important Implications

Peter Kilroy

Peter Kilroy is a British Academy postdoctoral fellow at King's College London. He holds PhD and MA degrees in cultural studies from the School of Fine Art, history of art and cultural studies at the University of Leeds, and a BA (hons.) in anthropology and cultural studies from the Schools of Anthropology and Politics at Queen's University Belfast.

The University of New South Wales recently found itself in a firestorm for reportedly encouraging students to use the terms "invasion," "occupation" or "colonisation" when discussing Captain Cook, who had hitherto often been described as "discovering" Australia in the 18th century, as part of the history of British "settlement."

However, behind this controversy lies a more nuanced debate. To the best of my knowledge, neither the university nor other similar bodies have claimed that there is one appropriate, neutral and value-free term. They merely suggest that "settlement" is "less appropriate" than "invasion" or the other suggested words—"colonisation" or "occupation"—all of which imply different historical and political positions and interpretations. Language matters, and emphasising a change of terminology—or, more importantly, emphasising that there is more than one position and term—demonstrates how much language is implicated in structures of power.

While not directly causal, there is a link between the language you use, the recognition of Indigenous peoples today and the redistribution of wealth, property and power to those peoples. It

"Discovery, settlement or invasion? The power of language in Australia's historical narrative," by Peter Kilroy, The Conversation, April 1, 2016. https://theconversation.com/discovery-settlement-or-invasion-the-power-of-language-in-australias-historical-narrative-57097. Licensed under a CC BY-ND 4.0 International.

is not merely about being "politically correct" nor is it restricted to the past.

Captain Cook's diaries

The key significance of the term "invasion" is that it demonstrates force, a lack of negotiation and Indigenous experience and resistance.

Captain Cook's diaries are complex and dense texts that resist easy summary. But from the very first encounter with Indigenous peoples they amply describe a state seeking to take charge of (a portion of) a continent and also the blunt force of physical violence.

Contrary to a common reading of terra nullius as "empty" or no-one's land, Cook and his advisers were eminently aware that "Australia" was not empty. The key point for them was whether property relations could be established between Indigenous people and the land via evident signs of occupation, architecture and/or agricultural cultivation. They could not or would not see such signs and so deemed the land amenable to possession.

No treaty was established (hence the move to establish one now), and the force of violence of Cook's encounters were repeated in generations of frontier wars, dispossession and murder. Historians might argue over the details and the extent of such force and violence (witness the so-called "history wars"), but there is ample evidence to attest to it. On that basis, "invasion" has a very different meaning to the much more benign sounding "settlement."

Undoing a historical trend, it also reframes the debate around Indigenous rather than "settler" experience. How different words produce different meanings is an important part of thinking critically about these debates. It is not about telling people what to think, but simply pointing out that what seems "natural" or beyond question is often not, and that language plays a key part in that process.

Terra nullius

The relative merits of these terms are arguably not as important as the fact that many Indigenous people demand, among other strategies, to take greater control of the language used to describe their experiences. It is a crucial sign of respect to listen to those voices (an important part of which is the recognition that there is no one "Indigenous" voice). This means establishing other conventions, for example capitalising Indigenous, highlighting the diversity of Indigenous peoples, and acknowledging Indigenous peoples as the owners and custodians of Australia.

To do so is not to relinquish critical thinking but to practice it in an environment of respectful dialogue that—at the very least—acknowledges both historical and ongoing injustices, and the relationship between them. The university is not banning language or debate. It is suggesting a preferred language within a broader context of respect, scholarship and political struggle.

Terra nullius was never an established, written doctrine explicitly laid out and followed by "settlers" or enshrined within law. It was a complex mix of philosophical ideas (going back to Hobbes, Locke and others)—loose cultural perceptions and shifting legal practices that were often not explicitly named. This makes it difficult to establish both what it was and how it might have been challenged.

Terra nullius was never about "emptiness." There are many "settler" accounts of signs of occupation, architecture and/or agricultural cultivation, albeit often witnessed on the margins of encampments, particularly in the early days. Those who did venture beyond their immediate environment recorded activities of agriculture and housing, but they often didn't understand them (digging up existing crops without realising that they had been deliberately planted, for example), or set the bar of inclusion above such activities (yes Indigenous people are planting but it is not "proper" agriculture). Or they wilfully ignored such activity for reasons of self-interest to stake their claim to a portion of land.

To that extent, these accounts, and those of Cook before them, present ample evidence to undermine their own claims to Australia. This is often the case under conditions of colonialism. Its beneficiaries are often remarkably adept at tolerating flawed logic at odds with direct evidence when it is in their interest to do so.

However, one of the greatest blows to the idea of terra nullius came from the "Mabo" Native Title decision in 1992 in which Eddie Mabo, a Torres Strait Islander—Australia's second Indigenous community, who live between Papua New Guinea and mainland Australia and in various diasporic communities across Australia—successfully fought for the recognition of their rights as the traditional owners of their land. One of the things that made Mabo's case successful was that it was easier to create an analogy between Torres Strait property relations or agricultural practices and those in European and Australian law than on mainland Australia.

Understanding the key importance of language, Mabo was able to argue that terra nullius did not make sense, even by the establishment's own standards. The great irony was that, because Australia had annexed the Torres Strait in the 1870s, the Mabo case could, in principle at least, set a precedent for the whole of the continent.

So language matters, and scholars in the social sciences and humanities have always been eminently aware of it. But that becomes particularly heightened when language, culture and politics meet in the classroom. In this context, language conventions and style sheets offer useful guidance for teachers and students, but they are the beginning of a discussion, not the end. Handled carefully, they are not just practical guides, much less a closing down of debate; they are an opening for critical thought.

Are College Campuses Too Politically Correct?

Overview: The Campus Setting Offers Both Reasons and Ramifications for Political Correctness

David A. Tomar

David A. Tomar is the editor-in-chief of The Best Schools *magazine. He is known for his 2010 article "The Shadow Scholar," which appeared in the* Chronicle of Higher Education, *and his subsequent 2012 memoir,* The Shadow Scholar: How I Made a Living Helping College Kids Cheat.

A re today's college students coddled, entitled, oversensitive, and ill-prepared for the real world?

Probably yes.

Should they have the power to call for change, demand inclusion, and advance equality?

Absolutely, they should.

But how to reconcile the two?

Somewhere between political correctness and bald-faced bigotry is the First Amendment. It protects our right to believe and say whatever we want just as it protects the rights of those who disgust us to believe and say whatever they want.

Today, more than ever before, college campuses are confronted with a problematic dilemma. What role must the university play in protecting the First Amendment? And what are its responsibilities to its students and faculty when the First Amendment facilitates expressions of hatred, insensitivity, or willful ignorance?

At what point does the drive for political correctness undermine this role? At what point does a failure to meet these responsibilities represent a threat to racial, gendered, and sexual harmony on campus?

"Do Inclusion and Sensitivity Threaten Free Speech?" by David A. Tomar for the Best School.org. Reprinted by permission.

These questions seem foremost on the minds of students, professors, and school administrators today.

But what is it that differentiates one university's policy of protection from another university's staunch commitment to free speech, the offended be damned?

Well, basically the same thing that separates Walmart, Urban Outfitters, Talbots, and Bloomingdale's from one another— the clientele.

Every college shares a single imperative: survival. Universities compete for students, ranking, endowments, funding, and reputation—though each does so with its own set of priorities and imperatives. Whether your university leads the annual party-school power rankings or derives its image from strong moral turpitude, whether it is known for its academic clout or draws its popularity from its accessibility, whether it is driven by a vaunted athletics program or the promise of diversity, every university has a brand.

Enter the hot topic of political correctness, at once a calling card for liberal activism and an epithet leveled by the conservative guard. As unrest ripples across campuses nationwide, and as demonstrations achieve a level of visibility that would have been impossible in the pre-Web era, the pressure on universities to respond has also never been greater.

But how each university responds is a matter of some variety. Those who believe there is a wholesale cultural thrust in which colleges are spinelessly yielding to the demands of an entitled and emotionally fragile generation of students are mistaken. So too are those who believe colleges are collectively and callously defying progress. The truth is somewhere in between and differs from one school to the next.

This is because, like most decisions a college must make, political correctness is an economic one.

P.C. Is a Dirty Word

Make no mistake, we are living in heated times. Cases like the shooting death of young Trayvon Martin in Miami-Gardens, Florida, and Michael Brown in Ferguson, Missouri—both unarmed black teenagers—and the emergence of the Black Lives Matter movement, have forced us to reevaluate race relations in a way not seen since the Civil Rights Era.

All evidence suggests that this is a conversation we need to have right now and that we must continue to have. As they have always been, college campuses are a hotbed for this kind of discourse. Young minds on all sides are willing and eager to throw down and pick up the gauntlet of debate.

But in a broader context, away from the sun-dappled mall of your college campus, the accusation of political correctness has become a powerful conceptual weapon designed to silence that conversation.

Peruse the Web for articles that accuse college campuses of stifling free speech in the name of political correctness. You'll find that many of these editorials have something in common: whether the discussion centers on racial discord, the permeation of sexual assault against women, the marginalization of the LGBT community, or the isolation of ethnic others—those who would otherwise defend themselves have been accused of doing so at the expense of free speech.

In a *Washington Post* column, conservative commentator George Will discusses what he perceives as political correctness run amok on college campuses, offering a condescending aside in which he implies that the concept of "Advanced Feminist Theory" is an oxymoron.

In a *New York Magazine* article, Jonathan Chait characterizes protests over racial discord at the University of Missouri as "an expression of a renewed left-wing hostility to freedom of expression."

Mitchell Blatt, in an article at *The Federalist*, says that "Universities are becoming more threatening for students, professors, public intellectuals, and free thinkers, but it is the politically correct social-justice fascists who are the most to blame."

Look closely at these examples, and at the level of discourse in general. These commentators are correct in asserting their right—and ours—to free speech. But a certain amount of misdirection cannot be overlooked. The political correctness backlash offers a quick exit from any honest discussion about racial disharmony, gender inequality, or the exclusion of marginalized groups.

The meaning of the "political correctness" has varied considerably both over the course of history and depending on who has wielded the phrase.

Check out *Washington Post*'s instructive and fascinating history on the phrase and its various fluctuations in meaning. Some of its earliest recorded instances are attributed to members of the American communist party in the '30s and '40s. They used the phrase to describe those political values that were thought to be ideologically right within the party.

In 1964, during a Convention of the United Auto Workers, President Lyndon B. Johnson said "I'm here to tell you that we are going to do those things which need to be done, not because they are politically correct, but because they are right," implying that political correctness was something that one engaged in merely to win elections.

The phrase emerged to describe an action or expression that was thought to be morally correct for the first time in the 1980s. This usage gradually morphed into a broader cultural movement for more inclusive thinking through language.

This led directly to a backlash in the 1990s wherein opponents of political correctness laid conceptual waste to the term. According to *The Washington Post*:

> "When the first President Bush declared that free speech was under siege by P.C. culture, 'mainstream America (began) to latch onto this term,' [Collins College history Professor] Burnett says. 'That's when 'political correctness' appeared on the nightly news.' More than 25 years later, you can still find it there. But

instead of describing a culture clash within academia, it's now a broad-brush insult directed against any ideological opponent."

Those who postured themselves as protectors of free speech found, in the P.C. movement, a decidedly convenient way to obstruct any ideological push for equal rights without ever having to voice their own biases. Its opponents were ultimately successful in recasting political correctness as language- and thought-policing.

As a consequence, political correctness is today most commonly bandied as an insult, leveled against liberals for what their conservative counterparts view as soft-headed oversensitivity so extreme as to trample on individual liberties.

The stigma of this phrase has become so effectively pronounced that few liberals will openly embrace the appellation, even if they embrace its underlying premise. Conservatives have emerged victorious from the semantic war over the phrase itself.

But the debate over political correctness is a smokescreen.

Legitimate Protest

The events on the University of Missouri campus have nothing to do with political correctness, neither the way that they unfolded nor the way they ultimately shook out.

This Fall, spurred by an open letter from Student Body President Payton Head over the permeation of racial disharmony on campus, members of the student body initiated an ongoing wave of demonstrations designed to force greater top-down recognition of the school's precarious climate. Tensions gradually boiled over, bringing widespread public attention to the protest and inciting variously crude responses from white-supremacy and neo-Nazi groups. Protesters called themselves Concerned Student 1950, named in recognition of the first year that the University of Missouri began admitting black students.

Concerned Student 1950 issued a list of demands to the University calling for greater representation of diversity among faculty and staff, a wider offering of culturally inclusive courses, and greater efforts to retain marginalized students. As it became clear that university president Timothy Wolfe was unprepared to negotiate this list of demands, the student group ultimately sought his ouster.

One of the group's more effective demonstrations was a mock campus tour that coincided with an actual tour of prospective enrollees and which highlighted the numerous locations around the university where racially charged incidents had occurred.

Among the more creative statements rendered by the opposition was a feces-swastika anonymously painted on the wall of a residence hall.

Now then, let us return to the claim that student protests are emblematic of political correctness run amok, or that a tenor of oversensitivity has stifled the prospect of open debate, or suppression of free speech. How should we classify the feces-swastika? Is that open debate, free speech, or good ol'-fashioned American candor, the kind that political correctness threatens with elimination?

When we conflate the over-sensitivity of our young adults with an actual demand for respect, change, acknowledgement, equality, or inclusiveness, we aren't just defending unfettered free speech. We are also legitimizing the messages of those who would resist change, equality, or inclusiveness. We're arguing that it's important for their messages to be heard...except that it isn't.

Those who express hatred have a right to do so but it is the responsibility of a healthy, functional, and progressive society to shout hatred down. This is not to stifle free speech. It is to demonstrate that certain speech, however legal, will not be culturally tolerated.

Free speech is very much intact, very much alive, and very much protected. This is America. You can say whatever you want, no matter how odd, embarrassing, or offensive. You can sit on your porch wearing a bathrobe and a toilet plunger for a hat, saying that same odd, embarrassing, or offensive stuff. The Constitution says so. (Well, it doesn't say the thing about the toilet plunger. Obviously, though, it's implied.)

But—and this is a big but—you must expect to face the consequences of your freedom, because, of course, everybody else is equally as free to tell you exactly how they feel about what you just said. This is true whether you're a raving derelict in an alleyway, a professor, or some combination of the two. Maybe in 1941, you could stand up in front of your lecture hall and speak disparagingly about women, or black people, or members of the LGBT community. You'd have gotten away with it, too, in the absence of those meddling kids. Those that you stood to offend, marginalize, or humiliate hadn't the collective voice or cultural visibility to do a thing about it.

Well that has changed quite significantly as college campuses—and society as a whole—have become more diverse and inclusive. That diversity has created quite the problem for those who wish to speak and act without consequence. Again, free speech tells us that we can say whatever we want. But today, with campuses serving the needs of an increasingly multicultural pool of students—many of them paying or borrowing exorbitant sums of money to be a part of their respective communities—insensitive, ignorant, and ethnocentric speech will have its consequences.

That is the price of free speech.

Safe Spaces and Trigger Warnings

Let's acknowledge the probability that some students are coddled, oversensitive, and bred (both by their parents and their Facebook friend groups) to silence opposing viewpoints.

The idea of the campus as a "Safe Space" is all well and good. But it also seems fairly counterintuitive to the idea that we are somehow preparing students for survival in a world brimming with real and pervasive danger.

In particular, if you consider bigotry, hatred, or good old-fashioned ignorance to be dangerous—and they certainly can be—you might consider never ever going on the Internet. Seriously, read the comment section following any article about anything.

Go read an article about how the high price of canola oil is ruining the average American's ability to bake muffins.

Then skip down to the comments section. Two comments in, somebody will blame Obama. Four comments in, somebody will refer to a fellow commenter whom they've never personally met as a "moron." Said fellow commenter will insult the original commenter's mother and then advise him to commit suicide. The next two dozen posts will devolve into seemingly unrelated diatribes targeting specific minorities with blanket observations and epithets.

And that's not even the real world. That's the virtual real world. In the real world, your senses will be constantly and unceasingly assaulted by ideas that you find offensive, by opinions that make you queasy, by worldviews that challenge your desire to see humanity as essentially good.

To this extent, your college does you a great disservice if it attempts to shelter you from these things. There will be no shelter when you sit on the train listening to the loud-mouth across the aisle spouting racial provocations into his cell phone. There will be no trigger warning when a presidential candidate tells you that all Mexicans are drug-peddling rapists. There will be no recourse when a drunken buffoon two barstools down from you explains to his strangely acquiescent friend that Bill Cosby was framed by a coven of fame-seeking succubi.

Well, there is one recourse. You can engage in rhetorically sound debate, if you think it's worth it (though it often isn't). But spending your college years wrapped in bubble-plastic will leave you ill-equipped to do anything other than be offended.

Nobody is questioning your right as a college student to be offended, nor to protest, nor to demand that your university take practical steps to ensure equal opportunity for all. But to demand that your university serve as a safe space seems a total misconception of higher education's purpose. The call for trigger warnings, the constant pinpointing of microaggressions, and the demand for action every time somebody even tangentially violates these principles are indeed evidence of a student body with a poor understanding of the world ahead of them.

The purpose of college is neither to coddle nor to comfort. It is to educate. If this education doesn't include at least some confrontation with that which makes you uncomfortable, with that which challenges your native assumptions, with that which is generally repulsive in the world, it has given you little exposure to the things that will be inescapable in your future.

It has also opened the door for any number of incidences which serve to largely discredit the push for progress.

There's the embarrassing snafu in which University of Missouri faculty member Melissa Click was captured on film assaulting a journalist who attempted to film a student demonstration. That... well that was just bad. It was bad, and misguided, and served to undermine a protest that, by all rights, should embrace all the visibility it can muster.

Click acted impulsively and with the intent of protecting her students, which has become a useful metaphor for those who would unfairly dismiss the Missouri protests as the temper-tantrums of sheltered children.

Other popularly cited examples of rampant sheltering are less incriminating but equally vulnerable to mockery.

Take, for instance, the University of Tennessee's widely derided approach to gender-identification sensitivity. The school's Office of Diversity and Inclusion published a statement urging teachers and students to respect gender neutrality by replacing the gender specific pronouns "he" and "she" with "ze." The University's desire to produce a more inclusive and accepting environment for its transgendered students is an admirable one.

Its approach, however, was remarkably oblivious to the ridicule and lampooning that would inevitably follow.

And follow they did. The language guide raised the hackles of self-proclaimed free speech defenders (never mind that it never achieved the status of a campus-wide policy initiative).

Ultimately, the university withdrew its language guide altogether amid a flurry of incorrectly reported claims that gender-specific pronouns had been banned on the campus. But it served as handy proof—if one was inclined to interpret it thusly—that the language police are coming for your words.

Then there was the case of the University of California, which in 2015 also became the subject of ridicule for including, among its faculty guidelines, a tool called "Recognizing Microaggressions and the Messages They Send."

The document explained that:

> Microaggressions are the everyday verbal, nonverbal, and environmental slights, snubs, or insults, whether intentional or unintentional, that communicate hostile, derogatory, or negative messages to target persons based solely upon their marginalized group membership.

Among the specific examples of microaggressions which were pulled out of context and made the subject of scorn, the guide advises against phrases like "America is the land of opportunity." It explains that such phrases assume a collective cultural experience which may not be true for members of marginalized groups. This advice obviously made a lot of Americans pretty angry.

Again, this was merely a guideline and never reached the point of policy-orientation. In fact, it doesn't even explicitly suggest that one must adhere to its conditions. It simply avails itself as a way of understanding what microaggressions are and how they can be avoided. It is also derived entirely from a 2010 text by Derald Wing Sue entitled *Microaggressions in Everyday Life: Race, Gender, and Sexual Orientation* and is thus not the work of the university itself. It is merely a reference.

As a measure for helping professors to become more respectful of classroom diversity, it probably wasn't the worst thing. As a PR tool, it kind of was the worst thing. Its specificity regarding the kinds of phrases and actions that one should avoid—sometimes useful and sometimes not so much—generally lends itself to parody.

It can also be readily constructed as evidence that one's freedom to be a jerk is somehow threatened. The efforts described above, well-intended though they might be, offer ammunition to the other side.

They also incline the very legitimate question, to what degree should we shield university-aged students from objectionable, even hateful, language? What if, by doing so, we deprive them of the experience and mental acuity to counteract this hatred? In what way, then, have we prepared them for a real world that is filled with a kind of hatred that can't be fixed by college education?

Basically, you'll have spent all of college bowling with bumpers, only to find that the real world is filled with gutters.

The Bottom Line Is, It's About the Bottom Line

But to dismiss every protest as the product of millennial entitlement is to strategically discredit the various progressive causes which often must be voiced through this medium.

For the record, today is no different than any other point in history. Students protest stuff. That's part of the campus experience for many young learners who are just beginning to define their beliefs and who harbor a sense that they can impact outcomes.

Your campus is the first community in which you actually feel you have a direct stake. It is a context where you feel that you can play a part in shaping the tenor, the atmosphere, the values, and the culture. And you are encouraged to do so, whether that means playing intramural ultimate frisbee, engaging in weekend neighborhood outreach programs, or picketing with signs and chanting things that rhyme.

If it is the last of these that you choose as your outlet for affiliation, your causes may vary dramatically. And in an era where marginalized groups have rightly taken steps to better define themselves and to more collectively defend their rights, the variance of subjects that might instigate protest is enormous.

So we've seen.

Students have a right to protest. And protests should be treated seriously to the extent that they deserve to be heard, acknowledged, overruled, or sustained.

But it would be an error in judgement to presume that this has anything to do with the validity of one student protest versus another. Whether a group is working to improve racial relations on a campus with an ingrained culture of racial hierarchy or campaigning for better vending machines in the student center, members of the group have something in common: they are customers.

The financial imperatives driving universities also have a marked impact on how they respond to campus protests. If it best serves your school's branding and image to acquiesce to student demands, than the latently racist professor, or the vile fraternity house, or the offending vending machine will be firmly disciplined. Then again, if it best serves the reputation of your campus to take a hardline stance on preserving cherished traditions and obstructing dissent, you will mince no words in condemning the disruptive few for detracting from the campus-wide harmony preferred by the silent majority.

For a prime example of the latter, take the words of Oklahoma Wesleyan President, Dr. Everett Piper. In the wake of the unrest in Missouri, Piper penned an open letter to nobody in particular noting that universities are not designed to be safe spaces. Quite to the contrary, he told his students that:

> Oklahoma Wesleyan is not a "safe place," but rather, a place to learn: to learn that life isn't about you, but about others; that the bad feeling you have while listening to a sermon is called guilt; that the way to address it is to repent of everything that's wrong with you rather than blame others for everything that's wrong with them. This is a place where you will quickly learn that you need to grow up.
>
> This is not a day care. This is a university.

Piper's harsh words are only ironic because Oklahoma Wesleyan maintains a student curfew, strictly forbids dancing, and punishes student parties with expulsion. So, y'know, it sounds a little bit like day care.

Given the strict code of moral hygiene dictated by Oklahoma Wesleyan, it seems pretty clear that its brand and image tie closely to a certain behavioral conformity. Piper has the luxury, possibly even a commercial imperative, to reassert his school's image as a house of order and decorum.

Then there are those universities that can afford—and perhaps may even benefit from—a few more dropouts. Again, such institutions need not concern themselves with sensitivity. Take Mount St. Mary's University in Maryland, for instance. A recent article from *Inside Higher Ed* reports on the contents of several leaked emails transmitted from University President Simon Newman to members of his faculty.

The President, a former private equity investment advisor executive, espoused a plan urging faculty to goad struggling students to drop out during their first semester. He explained to administrators that this tactic would effectively improve the appearance of the school's long-term retention rate by 4–5%.

Newman told his professors, "This is hard for you because you think of the students as cuddly bunnies, but you can't. You just have to drown the bunnies...put a Glock to their heads."

So on the one hand, universities shouldn't be such safe spaces that professors are not permitted to teach history, sociology, or political science with frankness and candor. On the other hand, they shouldn't be so unsafe that the president feels free to invoke this kind of imagery. Is it overly-sensitive to suggest that the president of a university shouldn't liken his students to cuddly bunnies that deserve to be drowned and shot? (And as a side question, what's wrong with this guy that he's blowing the brains out of bunnies?)

For just a moment, let's take a closer look at the claim (that I myself am guilty of sometimes believing) that college students are coddled, entitled, needy, and oversensitive. Let's consider how many of them will leave college in hopeless debt, how many of them will endure this experience without meaningful academic support, how many of them will have entered their campus as overlooked minorities, underserved immigrant populations, or marginalized cultural subgroups. Their experiences are not the gentle and nurturing ones that you imagine.

In reality, students must often choose their educational path by virtue of affordability and accessibility. Sometimes, these priorities overshadow the desire to live on a campus where one feels culturally accepted or welcome. For students who fall into this category, who find that their experiences are not only overlooked by their universities but that they are largely invisible, is it not reasonable to attempt to carve out some cultural space? To question their right to do so—which seems largely the prerogative of P.C. critics—is itself an act which aims to curtail free speech. In other words, freedom works both ways and so does suppression.

Political Correctness is not some powerful and sweeping movement designed to homogenize public discourse or to promote thought control. It is exactly the opposite. It is a symptom of hierarchy and proof of the eventuality that those at the bottom will strive for empowerment. That this is happening in colleges across America reminds us that our campuses are increasingly diverse, and that such diversity will instigate change. It is not, as George Will calls it, evidence of "campuses so saturated with progressivism that they celebrate diversity in everything but thought."

Critics of Will's ilk should be happy to know that colleges remain, today, as driven by capitalism as ever before, perhaps more so.

Even those progressive demonstrations which ultimately succeed do so as a consequence of some larger financial practicality.

Indeed, before you look to the resignation of Missouri's president—which came to pass in November of 2015—as evidence that political correctness is in command on the old Mizzou campus, you should know that his departure only became a matter of inevitability after the football team joined protesters.

Former Missouri University president Wolfe has expressed no regret for failing to reign in an increasingly problematic racial tension but has been critical of the athletic program's decision to boycott all upcoming games until his resignation. The first of those upcoming games was to have been a contest with BYU. Had Missouri forfeited the match, its athletics department would have been contractually obligated to furnish its would-be opponent with $1 million.

This cost alone created a kind of pressure on the university's president that no amount of political correctness ever could.

Wolfe blames the football program, and not the fact that he had lost control over his campus, for his departure. He was probably not wrong. Clearly, money, not race—and most assuredly not political correctness—made this change inevitable.

Political correctness is a concept brandished with so much hostility that incidents suggesting its impracticality are trumpeted as evidence that free speech is dead.

This is not what's happening. Campuses that depend on their appearance as bastions of liberal thinking will allow visible and voluble student groups to control their actions. Campuses that exude conservative dignity as a matter of branding will quell any such resistance firmly, decisively, and without transparency.

The debate over political correctness is a particularly useful diversion from the thoughtful discussion that we might otherwise have every time a student group raises a good point—or every time a student group raises a bad point, for that matter. So much has the phrase "politically correct" become anathematized that its invocation prevents us from determining which controversies deserve recognition and which truly are evidence of a coddled and entitled student body.

Indeed, as of this writing, we are in the midst of a presidential campaign season wherein the phrase "politically correct" is used as a weapon against any utterance in favor of inclusion, in opposition to bigotry, in contention with established patterns of discrimination.

All this talk about political correctness and whether it has become so rampant as to reduce free speech on campus is a boatload of libertarian fear-mongering. There isn't really a concerted movement on campus to stifle free speech or to silence opposing viewpoints. But students do see themselves as customers and if they see something objectionable about the product they're paying for, they will say so.

Universities have the right to respond however they desire, but the impact of that response on the end consumer is a major factor.

It's easy to call it "political correctness run amok," as though the students raising signs outside administration buildings are somehow the ones in control. But they aren't. They are at the mercy of their universities, and their future employers, and their student loans, and the harsh realities of life after graduation.

Protest is really the only recourse they have.

Administrators and Students Are Too Concerned with Political Correctness

Daniel J. Mitchell

Daniel J. Mitchell is a member of the Foundation for Economic Education Faculty Network and a senior fellow at the Cato Institute. He has written for a wide range of well-known publications and holds a PhD from George Mason University.

A few years ago, I put together an amusing collection of stories comparing truly bizarre examples of political correctness and bureaucratic idiocy in the United States and United Kingdom.

I was especially impressed (in a you-must-be-joking fashion) that a British job placement office got in trouble for discrimination because they sought "reliable" and "hard-working" applicants. Sounds impossible to believe, but consider the fact that the EEOC bureaucracy in the U.S. went after a trucking company because it didn't want to employ drunk drivers.

And I've shared jaw-dropping reports of anti-gun political correctness in American schools, as well as a proposal to ban skinny models in Britain.

Let's expand on this collection of horror stories.

Reason reports that some bureaucrats in New York City think that it is sexual harassment for a professor to base grades in part on effort and classroom behavior.

> A professor at the City University of New York's Brooklyn College was ordered to make changes to his syllabus because it amounted to sexual harassment. The professor, David Seidemann, has refused to comply, and for good reason. ... a university administrator expressed three grievances about the syllabus. First, and most quizzically, the grading portion of the syllabus

suggests sexual harassment. It reads, "Class deportment, effort etc. ... 10% (applied only to select students when appropriate)." ... Seidemann told me in an email that his department chair said "the 10% section could be construed as a prelude to sexual harassment," and had to be changed at once. This order apparently came from the Director of Diversity Investigations and Title IX Enforcement. In the course of Seidemann's interactions with the director, he realized something quite stunning: there was no record of anyone actually complaining about the syllabus. The university had apparently launched this investigation on its own. ...The professor refused to meet with the Director of Diversity Investigations, preferring to talk via email so that the conversation could be documented. This eventually caused the director to abandon the investigation: the matter is now officially closed, according to Seidemann. The professor is pleased with the result, but little else.

If you read the entire story, it appears that the bureaucrats decided that "effort" could be interpreted as an invitation for female students to trade sex for higher grades. At least I think that's the implication.

In which case, there must have been rampant sexual harassment when I was young because our report cards in elementary school always included our teachers' assessment of our "effort." And all the way through college, I periodically had classes in which grades were based in part on "participation."

I guess I was so young and naive that I didn't realize my teachers and professors were inviting me to offer sex for grades (my grades often were low enough that it was probably best I didn't run the risk of having them go even lower).

More seriously, I'm glad the professor stood up against the absurd accusations put forth by the diversity bureaucrats. I especially like that he insisted on having everything occur via email so he couldn't be victimized by the selective memory of some pencil pushers who probably try to justify their comfortable sinecures by claiming an occasional scalp.

Bureaucrats in Knoxville, Tennessee, also seem to be amazingly skilled at seeing sexual harassment where it doesn't exist.

The student, Keaton Wahlbon, had to take a geology quiz featuring the following question: "What is your lab instructor's name? (if you don't remember, make something good up)." Wahlbon followed the instructions: he didn't remember, so wrote down the first generic girl name that came to mind— Sarah Jackson. Unbeknowst to Wahlbon, Sarah Jackson is a real person: a pornographic model. Of course, there are hundreds (thousands?) of other Sarah Jacksons in the world, and Wahlbon had no idea that his lab instructor would interpret his answer in such a specific and malicious manner. His answer was marked "inappropriate" and he received a grade of zero on the quiz. Wahlbon appealed to his professor, Bill Deane, but Deane maintained that Wahlbon had committed sexual harassment. Wahlbon contacted the head of department because, well, that's nonsense. ... no resolution has been reached yet. But according to *The Knoxville News Sentinel*, the university is now investigating the matter as if a complaint had been filed—even though no one has taken such an action.

Wow, this is surreal. Let's assume, for the sake of argument, that Mr. Wahlbon was thinking of the pornographic model when he wrote "Sarah Jackson" on the quiz. How is this sexual harassment? I don't claim to be an expert on such matters, but I'm under the impression that harassment occurs when someone with power in a relationship makes some sort of sexual advance (or even tells a dirty joke). So how can a student harass a teacher? Or even a teacher's lab instructor?

You can say that Wahlbon is guilty of displaying bad taste, but then we get to the issue of whether he actually meant the Sarah Jackson. If it was a more uncommon name (such as Jenna Jameson, the famous Republican-supporting porn star), then you could safely assume (though not legally prove) that he intended to make a boorish joke. But is the Sarah Jackson so famous that it's safe to think that's who Wahlbon had in mind? For what it's worth, I never heard of that Sarah Jackson (though I once dated a girl with that name).

By the way, the British have similarly brainless people in their nation.

Though they express their political correctness in non-sexual ways (what a surprise), such as the principal who has banned running on the playground.

> The headmaster of Hillfort Primary School in Liskeard, Dr Tim Cook, introduced the ban to prevent the little blighters injuring themselves. Instead, kids at Hillfort can blow off steam at playtime by playing with Lego, Jenga, and even dancing, as part of the school's plan to reduce "negative behaviours." Cook has responded by reassuring parents that their children are not completely prohibited from running—they are just not allowed to run across the playground. Have the nippers been given a small area to run around instead? Getting dizzier and dizzier as they charge about in circles? …Arguing that the ban is for safety reasons is pathetic. It's running, not sword-swallowing. Grazed knees are part of growing up, and do not, or at least should not, result in lawsuits.

Fortunately, British parents seem a bit more sensible than their bureaucratic overlords. They're petitioning to allow their kids to… gasp…do more than walk on the playground during recess.

There's also lunacy in Australia. And since I'm a parent, I'm especially horrified about what happened to a father who wanted to protect his stepdaughter from sexting.

> A man who found out that his 15-year-old stepdaughter was sexting her boyfriend proceeded to download the evidence to bring it to the school and the police to ask them to intervene. … Intervene they did. Now the dad has been convicted on child pornography charges and placed on the sex offender registry. This, despite the judge understanding exactly why the man, Ashan Ortell, 57, held onto the images. "There is no suggestion of any exploitation of them by anybody," ruled Judge Jane Patrick, over in Australia, which is becoming as daffy as the United States.

"You made no attempt to conceal the images. In fact, you were so concerned that you contacted the authorities about the images."

If you read the entire story, I'm guessing that the cops went after the dad because he was badgering them for not doing anything about his stepdaughter. And I sympathize with the cops for choosing not to make a big deal out of two teenagers sexting, but did they really have to go after the guy for having the images when nobody thinks he had any unsavory intent or motives?

Keep in mind that this took place in the nation that awarded workers compensation to a woman who injured herself while having sex and also threatened fines against companies that pointed out the downside of a carbon tax.

All that being said, Australia is still my top choice for where to go if (when?) America suffers a Greek-style fiscal and economic collapse.

P.S. I've come across lots of crazy government decisions in my time, so I'm not surprised by today's material. Though since I mentioned Greece, that government deserves some sort of prize for subsidizing pedophiles and demanding stool samples before letting entrepreneurs set up online companies.

And let's not forget that European courts that have ruled that there's an entitlement to free soccer broadcasts and a right to satellite TV. About as nutty as the Finnish court that ruled there's a right to broadband access, and as crazy as the Bolivian decision that there's a human right to receive stolen property.

P.P.S. In his speech to the 2008 Democratic Convention, former Massachusetts Governor Deval Patrick said "Government, as Barney Frank likes to say, is simply the name we give to the things we choose to do together."

If that's true, then the above examples show that we "choose" to do some really foolish things. In reality, as Glenn Reynolds of Instapundit reminds us, we don't choose.

On-Campus Free Speech Continues to Diminish as a Result of Political Correctness

Greg Lukianoff

Greg Lukianoff is an attorney and the president and CEO of the Foundation for Individual Rights in Education (FIRE). The widely published author wrote Unlearning Liberty: Campus Censorship and the End of American Debate *and* Freedom From Speech, *and he was the executive producer of the documentary* Can We Take a Joke?

2015 will be remembered as a year in which campus free speech issues took center stage, receiving extensive coverage in outlets like *The New York Times*, *Wall Street Journal*, *The Atlantic*, *Slate*, *Vox*, and *Salon*. Even President Obama voiced concerns about the lack of debate on college campuses.

For those of us who have been fighting campus censors for years, it's hard not to ask: "Where has everyone been?"

My organization, the Foundation for Individual Rights in Education (FIRE), has been defending freedom of expression on campus since 1999. We can attest that free speech, open inquiry, and academic freedom have always been threatened on campus by one force or another, even long before we were founded.

Most people are familiar with the supposed heyday of political correctness of the 1980s and 90s, but there is a popular misconception that speech codes and censorship were defeated in the courts of law and public opinion by the mid-90s. In reality, the threats to campus speech never went away. Before examining what has changed to alarm the public—rightfully—about the state of open discourse in higher education, it's important to note what hasn't changed.

"Campus Free Speech Has Been in Trouble for a Long Time," by Greg Lukianoff, Cato Institute, January 4, 2016. ©The Cato Institute 2016. Used By Permission.

Speech Codes and Political
Correctness Never Went Away

Scholars, including First Amendment expert Robert O'Neil, claim that politically correct speech codes were given a "decent burial" in the mid-90s. But despite being repeatedly defeated in court, speech codes became the rule rather than the exception on campus.

FIRE has been tracking and rating speech codes at hundreds of colleges and universities since 2006. Eight years ago, 75 percent of the institutions we surveyed maintained policies worthy of FIRE's "red light" rating, meaning they clearly and substantially restricted freedom of speech. Since then, the percentage of schools with red light speech codes has steadily declined each year.

This good news is due, at least in part, to FIRE's aggressive campaigning and lawsuits. Over the past few years, the number of campuses with red light policies decreased from 62.1 percent (2013) to 55.2 percent (2015). And, in FIRE's 2016 speech code report, that figure is below 50 percent (49.3 percent) for the first time. Unfortunately, this may be only a temporary high-water mark; pressure from students and the federal government makes the resurgence of speech codes almost inevitable.

The past 15 years are rife with examples of speech-policing. There are the classic political correctness cases, such as the 2004 incident in which a University of New Hampshire student was evicted from his dorm for posting flyers joking that freshman women could lose the "Freshman 15" by walking up the dormitory stairs. In 2009, Yale University students were told they shouldn't quote F. Scott Fitzgerald, and Bucknell University students were forbidden from handing out "Obama Stimulus Dollars."

But many cases do not follow the "PC" mold and just involve old-fashioned abuses of power. Examples include the University of Wisconsin-Stout's censorship of a professor's "Firefly" poster, Central New Mexico Community College's shutdown of a student newspaper for publishing a "Sex Issue," and former Valdosta State University student Hayden Barnes' unjust expulsion for protesting a parking garage (which led to an eight-year-long legal battle that finally concluded in 2015).

Federal Antidiscrimination Law as the Secret Engine of Campus Censorship

Some trends that long precede (and may explain) the current threats to campus free speech include the massive expansion of the bureaucratic class at universities, which officially began outnumbering the number of full-time instructors in 2005, and the rise of the "risk management" industry, which makes a fortune teaching universities how to avoid lawsuits by regulating almost every aspect of student life.

This brings us to the institution that is perhaps most responsible for exacerbating the problems of speech codes and hair-trigger censorship: the Department of Education's Office for Civil Rights (OCR).

By the late 1980s, colleges were adopting "anti-harassment" codes that restricted protected speech. In the mid-1990s, the campus speech code phenomenon converged with the expansion of federal anti-discrimination law by the Department of Education's Office for Civil Rights (OCR). OCR encouraged and even required harassment codes, and although its guidance tried to "balance" the need for these codes with the First Amendment, by the time FIRE was founded in 1999, universities were using the "federal government made me do it" excuse to justify even the most laughably unconstitutional speech codes.

In 2003, in perhaps its most redeeming moment, OCR issued a letter clarifying that it has no power to mandate that universities— public or private—police speech that is protected under the First Amendment. OCR explained that public universities, which are bound by the First Amendment, cannot ban merely offensive speech. And if private universities, which are not bound by the First Amendment (except in California through the Leonard Law), pass such speech codes, OCR made clear that they can in no way argue that the federal government forced their hand.

This message was never fully accepted by campus administrators, who wanted expansive speech codes, or by risk managers, who believed it was safer to discourage offensive speech than face a lawsuit. Nonetheless, the 2003 letter did help defuse an old excuse.

Unfortunately, the Department of Education under the Obama administration has been much more aggressive, granting itself new powers and redefining harassment in such broad language that virtually any offensive speech could be considered a matter of federal oversight.

In May 2013, OCR and the Department of Justice (DOJ) entered into a resolution agreement with the University of Montana that the agencies deemed "a blueprint for colleges and universities throughout the country." This "blueprint" mandates an extraordinarily broad definition of sexual harassment: "any unwelcome conduct of a sexual nature," including "verbal conduct"—i.e., speech. The blueprint holds that this conduct need not be "objectively offensive" to constitute sexual harassment. This means that if a listener takes offense to any sex- or gender-related speech, no matter how irrationally or unreasonably, the speaker has engaged in sexual harassment. Additionally, the final UM policy reviewed and approved by OCR and DOJ as part of their resolution agreement goes beyond policing sex-related speech by also prohibiting discriminatory harassment on the basis of 17 different categories, including "political ideas."

Treating this resolution agreement as a "blueprint" puts public universities in an impossible situation: violate the First Amendment or risk investigation and the possible loss of federal funding.

OCR backed away from its characterization of the Montana agreement as a "blueprint" in a November 2013 letter to me. But unlike the clarification it issued in 2003, OCR has never communicated this to universities. As a result, as universities revise their sexual misconduct policies, they now include the blueprint's definition of sexual harassment. There can be little doubt that the number of institutions doing so will only increase until OCR clarifies that it cannot require universities to adopt such a definition.

OCR is unlikely to forego unconstitutional speech-policing any time soon. In October, OCR announced that it would open a Title IX investigation into the University of Mary Washington after students filed a complaint about the school's handling of sexist and racist Yik Yak posts. If this investigation leads to new federal "guidance" on colleges' responsibility to police students' social media activity, even more protected campus speech could be threatened.

What Has Changed: Students Using Their Free Speech to Limit Free Speech

The biggest and most noticeable change in campus censorship in recent years has been the shift in student attitudes. Today, students often demand freedom from speech rather than freedom of speech.

Media coverage of the campus free speech crisis exploded in 2014 after a rash of "disinvitations"—student and faculty attempts to disinvite controversial speakers from campus, including former Secretary of State Condoleezza Rice and International Monetary Fund head Christine Lagarde.

Attention from the media has increased as more student-led efforts have gained popularity, such as demands for "trigger warnings" and "safe spaces," and efforts to police so-called "microaggressions." Critiquing PC culture is nothing new for conservative outlets, but even left-leaning authors at the *New Republic*, *The Nation*, *New York Magazine*, and *The New York Times* have been writing extensively about how these trends reflect very new, often alarming student attitudes about open discourse.

In my 15 years at FIRE, students have historically been the most reliably pro-free-speech constituency on campus. Students often showed more common sense than the professoriate, and certainly much more than the administrators.

But when stories about campus race-related protests inundated the news in the fall of 2015, I knew something had changed. It began when students at Wesleyan University demanded that the school's primary student newspaper be defunded after it published a student op-ed that was critical of the Black Lives Matter movement. Shortly after, Wesleyan's student government unanimously approved a resolution that will tentatively cut the paper's printing budget by half.

Things escalated when I saw firsthand that Yale students were demanding the resignations of two faculty members for sending out an email that questioned whether universities should tell students what they should or shouldn't wear as Halloween costumes. Then, just days later, student protests at the University of Missouri soured when protesters manhandled a student journalist.

These protests put First Amendment defenders and free speech advocates like me in a somewhat difficult position. Of course, I'm supportive of students exercising their free speech rights. Indeed, I find it refreshing that students have overcome their oft-diagnosed apathy towards serious social issues. However, it's distressing that many of the protesters are using their free speech to demand limitations on others' free speech. The irony of these demands was particularly prominent at the University of Missouri, where FIRE recently helped pass a state law making it illegal to limit free speech activities on public university campuses to tiny zones. This new law helped make the Mizzou students' protests possible. But in a twist, the protesters created their own free speech exclusion zone to prevent media from covering the protest.

Now student protestors at at least 75 American colleges and universities have released lists of demands "to end systemic and structural racism on campus." Although this is a laudable goal, a troubling number of these demands would prohibit or chill campus speech.

For example, many of the demands try to make the expression of racial bias, which is generally protected speech, a punishable offense. At Johns Hopkins University, protesters demand "impactful repercussions" for anyone who makes "Black students uncomfortable or unsafe for racial reasons." Similarly, protesters at

Georgia's Kennesaw State University demand "strong repercussions and sanctions" for those who commit "racist actions and racial bias on campus." And Emory University protestors want a bias response reporting system and sanctions for even "unintentional" acts or behaviors, including "gestures."

Others go as far as to mandate that universities forbid "hate speech." At Missouri State University, protesters demand that administrators announce a "commitment to differentiating 'hate speech' from 'freedom of speech.'" Protesters at Dartmouth College want "a policy with serious consequences against hate speech/ crimes (e.g. Greek house expelled for racist parties)." Similarly, student protesters at the University of Wyoming demand that the code of conduct be revised to hold students accountable for hate speech, complete with "a detailed reporting structure."

The evidence that today's students value freedom of speech less than their elders is not just anecdotal. In October, Yale University's William F. Buckley, Jr. Program released a survey that found that 51 percent of U.S. college students favor campus speech codes, and that 72 percent support disciplinary action against "any student or faculty member on campus who uses language that is considered racist, sexist, homophobic or otherwise offensive." These troubling results were echoed by a November 2015 global survey from Pew Research Center finding that a whopping 40 percent of U.S. millennials [ages 18–34] believe the government should be able to punish speech offensive to minority groups (as compared to only 12 percent of the Silent generation [70–87 year-olds], 24 percent of the Boomer generation [51–69 year-olds], and 27 percent of Gen Xers [35–50 year-olds]).

Conclusion

Thankfully, through old strategies and new ones, we can improve the climate for free speech on campus. Just one student or professor can protect free expression for thousands, or even hundreds of thousands, by filing a lawsuit against his or her school with the help of FIRE's Stand Up For Speech Litigation Project. SUFS is undefeated so far and has resulted in seven settlements that send the clear message to institutions that it will be expensive to ignore their obligations under the First Amendment. What's more, with every speech-protective judgment, it becomes harder for administrators to defend themselves with "qualified immunity," which shields individuals from personal liability where the law isn't clear.

Litigation might also be our best shot at forcing OCR to step back from its efforts to coerce institutions into adopting unconstitutional policies. Clearer and narrower policies than OCR's May 2013 definition of "sexual harassment" have been struck down in court on numerous occasions. But until institutions see a real threat of an expensive judgment against them for overbroad harassment policies, they'll continue to be motivated by the threat of OCR pulling their funding for what it seems to consider underbroad policies—i.e., colleges will err on the side of prohibiting protected expression.

And because money talks, alumni should withhold donations to institutions that break the law or renege on promises to respect students' and professors' rights. And of course, anyone can contact his or her legislators and ask them to support bills—like the ones FIRE helped enact in Missouri and Virginia—that ensure students may fully exercise their free speech rights on public campuses statewide.

These strategies may motivate schools to make quick changes, but free speech advocates know that long-lasting progress comes through cultural change. How do we teach a generation about the value of free expression when speech is too often presented as a problem to be overcome, rather than part of the solution to many social ills? This is our great challenge, and it must be faced with both determination and creativity if the always-fragile right of freedom of speech is to endure.

"Safe Space" Is a Valuable Element of the Campus Setting

Jennifer Wallin-Ruschman and Mazna Patka

Jennifer Wallin-Ruschman is an assistant professor at the College of Idaho. Mazna Patka is a professor at Governors State University in Illinois.

Abstract

Safe spaces have the potential to become prefigurative groups that aim to create social change. The idea of a safe space as a place separate and sheltered from dominant culture to mobilize for social change has gained traction in a number of academic and practical areas. However, safe spaces have the ability to be both progressive and regressive. To guide our discussion we utilize the concept of community-diversity dialectic to address the tension between these forces within two settings. First we discuss research in an upper level college course rooted in feminist praxis. Then we discuss a faith community's use of adaptive liturgy with parishioners with intellectual disabilities. Following this discussion, we offer a new term, "critical collective spaces," to better capture the work done in these spaces. We offer this alternative label to move popular and academic discourse away from debating about how "safe" these spaces are (or are not) and toward a more nuanced discussion of the community-diversity dialectic and other tensions within these spaces. Our overall intention is to generate dialogue on the regressive and progressive aspects of these locations and to inform the activism and community building process within prefigurative politics more broadly.

Introduction

"Safe spaces"[1] are literal and figurative areas and processes that are sometimes removed from the control of a dominant group to facilitate the development of networks and skill building among individuals to create social change. Like prefigurative groups, individuals in safe spaces engage in consciousness raising, community building, and political mobilization (Collins, 1999; Polletta, 1999). While prefigurative groups are involved in the creation of spaces and processes to develop alternative ways of imagining and enacting a model of a new and better society (Armstrong, 2002), they may initially develop through safe spaces. Safe spaces may develop into a prefigurative group with shared values and goals, and later as prefigurative groups that engage in social action. We contend that safe spaces are a critical yet underexplored facet of prefigurative politics.

Prefigurative groups, particularly early in their development, may limit membership to create safe spaces (Polletta, 1999). Small intimate groups may allow for free expression when compared to larger and/or more diverse group configurations (Polletta, 1999). For example, women's only groups may be limited to women and disability groups may be limited to people with disabilities; these configurations allow for more intimacy and can offer enhanced possibilities for free expression (Collins, 1999; Polletta, 2002).

Prefigurative groups outline their processes for realizing a better society (Maeckelbergh, 2011), which requires building a community. Working to develop community may necessitate that group members build close relationships involving personal sharing. The process of building connections among members may reveal differences in life experiences, perceptions, or goals. Thus, a primary tension in prefigurative groups may exist between building community and the need for a sense of individual autonomy (Hardt, 2013); the focus on building community to achieve the group's goals may overshadow diversity among group members. Alternatively, overly focusing on diversity may hinder the development of sense of community.

The limitations of focusing on community are evident in the safe space tactics developed in feminist consciousness raising groups in the second wave of the women's movement (Ferree & Hess, 2000) and the gay liberation movement (Armstrong, 2002). Both movements have been criticized for focusing on the needs of upper and middle class whites (Armstrong, 2002; Ferree & Hess, 2000). Similarly, during the civil rights movement Black Southern churches functioned as safe spaces, which were removed from the control of white Americans and provided a physical space for African Americans to develop a network and strategize (Polletta, 1999).

A safe space intends to move out of the control of the dominant group and allow physical and/or figurative room for identity development, social support, emotional connection, and sense of community, and facilitate development of critical consciousness (Collins, 1999; Tatum, 2003). While originally conceptualized as existing within social movements, the idea of safe spaces has been taken up by those outside of social movements. The application of safe spaces within fields such as education has increased the visibility of safe spaces but it has also been met with critique and backlash (see Agness, 2015; Noonan, 2015). We argue that safe spaces share many processes and tensions with prefigurative groups. Further, we see safe spaces as one aspect of prefigurative politics. Safe spaces may transform into a prefigurative group that shifts into the view of mainstream society to create social change (Polletta, 1999). Thus, safe spaces can be used to create a foundation for a movement through recruitment and development of its members (Gamson, 1991). We believe that by explicitly linking the ideas of safe spaces and prefigurative politics we can expand the understanding of both, including the benefits and challenges of each.

Although underexplored in the social sciences literature, safe spaces are a key tactic for social movements both in the past and present day. Consequently, the formations and processes involved in safe spaces vary widely within practice. We seek to honor the historical and present use of safe spaces by prefigurative and other social movements while also bringing a critical lens to their use to better understand their potential benefits and challenges. We have learned from our time in community safe spaces, both those presented here and others in which we have engaged as activists. Our goal is to offer reflections on the use of safe spaces, their connection to broader prefigurative politics, and ideas for addressing some of the challenges we have identified in working within safe spaces. However, we acknowledge our definitions of safe spaces and prefigurative politics do not capture the full breadth of their practice and that our suggestions may have limited utility outside of this manuscript. Our intention is to open a dialogue on these issues that extends beyond this special thematic section and stimulates further exploration. Herein, we present research on the community-diversity dialectic and share our experiences with and research on safe spaces in university classrooms and community disability groups.

[...]

Safe Spaces in College Classrooms

The first author conducted a participant observation[2] at an urban university in a senior capstone course[3] focused on developing feminist consciousness. The six-hour course integrated classroom time with community engagement where students conducted "rap sessions" with groups of adolescent girls in community settings. The course content was interdisciplinary in nature but concentrated on understanding issues of gender oppression, particularly in relation to adolescent girls. The course instructor was highly committed to Critical and Feminist Pedagogies and utilized aspects of each, including: group work, discussion, focusing on the intersection of social identities, and voice. Class time occurred seated in a circle and was spent building community through activities, such as daily check-ins and practicing skills necessary for conducting the community engagement component of the course. The course involved self-reflection and activities, such as identity mapping, which facilitated students' ability to understand how broad socio-political structures influence them and the adolescent girls they worked with in the community. The course consisted of 15 women and one man and students were diverse in regard to race, age and sexual orientation. Following completion of the course 10 semi-structured interviews were conducted with women students. A modified version of the listening guide (Gilligan, Spencer, Weinberg, & Bertsch, 2003) was used for analysis.

Safe for Whom?

In our work in college classrooms that utilize Feminist and Critical pedagogical techniques, the process of demarcating a space and separating it from some outside "other" is seen through a number of practices; for example, in the capstone we observed the instructor closing the door to "protect the space." That said, the biggest challenges to the idea of "safe for whom" came from inside the group.

In individual interviews with students, months after completion of the course, they suggested some degree of power imbalance had existed among students in the course. One of the few older students in the course talked of "not fitting in." Another repeatedly stated how much she enjoyed and learned from the course but also expressed how "hard" the class had been and how on some days she "just didn't want to be there." This same student expressed her frustration:

> For me it's difficult sometime being the only women of color sitting in the classroom, because, usually when we talk about what's happening in the world we're talking about it from a dominant perspective. Well that's not me and so, to find a way in which I fit into all of this, it's not always easy.

In the heterogenous environment of the college classroom, the ideal of a safe space was not always realized. In fact, students with more areas of marginalization or students that were the only representative of a group seemed to particularly struggle.

Another theme centered on the emotional toll of being in a classroom that utilized aspects of safe space ideology. A white traditional age student in the course said:

> … when we were talking about like social mapping, I was like hell no, identity circle, that was so tolling … It was like, yes this was unifying, but it was also taking a toll on my psychological well-being. Luckily I still see a therapist regularly so I got to be like I'm tired, I'm drained, help.

While some activities in the course worked to build community, these same activities stretched individuals' abilities to cope. Literature on safe spaces has generally not discussed these potential regressive effects of such experiences on individuals, particularly those that have more traumatic histories or limited resources (e.g., therapy, social support; Wallin-Ruschman, 2014).

Safe From What?

To justify the need for a safe space, an environment has to be labeled as problematic. The relatively heterogeneous nature of the safe space in college classrooms makes the defined outside other fairly generic. Because there are people of various social locations within the classroom, one does not see the same division one might see in a more homogeneous space. In the classroom, dominant culture and mainstream media were labeled as the other to which the space is defined in opposition. When defined in this way the space becomes an area to foster critical consciousness that critiques norms and values of dominant culture and mainstream media. A student in the capstone discussed the hostility of the dominant culture by stating:

> I mean you have to create a safe space for people to say what they feel, to think what they feel, because I think a lot of people struggle with allowing themselves just to think about something without beating themselves up.

The quote suggests that the class played an important role in helping students transfer emotions and thoughts that previously felt deviant into acceptable thoughts and feelings.

While defining the safe space in opposition to dominant culture can foster the development of critical consciousness, it can also be regressive. First, placing all "badness" on an outside other does not allow individuals to work through the internal and even unconscious biases they have developed through living in the dominant culture. Second, labeling and critiquing all mainstream media can become exhausting. This changing orientation can take some of the fun and humor out of previously enjoyed activities. A woman from the capstone class articulated her dissonance:

> … there's TV shows and there's music that I like on some levels that I now have trouble listening to … and that's where a lot of these negative stereotypes are being propagated is in like mainstream music and videos … I know that that's offensive and not okay, but I still really like this song …

Safe for What Activities?

The creation of classroom guidelines was used to negotiate what activities were appropriate for the space. While this activity seemed to put students at ease and facilitate community building, it was unclear how much it actually changed the tenor of the class. Despite students agreeing to step up (i.e., if they are usually quiet, challenge themselves to talk) or step down (i.e., if they are usually talkative challenge themselves to listen more), the same students spoke from day to day and some almost never verbally participated during class. Another common guideline raised was engaging in dialogue. The process of dialogue is important because it allows for hearing others perspective and is a fundamental driver of critical consciousness development (Wallin-Ruschman, 2014). However, the very idea of dialogue hints that there are diverse perspectives in the room. Students seemed to struggle with the community-diversity dialectic and perceive the presence of diversity or disagreement as threatening to their sense of community.

In the capstone course any area of disagreement was generally perceived negatively. This was the case even when the conflict was a part of the participatory decision-making process. One student was surprised when the structure of the course led to disagreement:

> I was surprised that people did not agree and there was just so much back and forth going on. But I don't know, maybe they were just very opinionated and they were advocating for themselves I guess. But it was just really hard for us to, like, find common ground on a lot of topics.

This woman and a number of other participants stated that they preferred to avoid conflict whenever possible. Additionally, dialogue in the class itself was often viewed as rife with tension. Participants preferred that everyone "get along" and agree. This tendency does not leave room for critical dialogue and limits progressive capacities including the ability to tolerate ambivalence and conflict (Haaken, Wallin-Ruschman, & Patange, 2012).

[...]

Notes

1. We place the term safe space in quotations here because we acknowledge this is a problematic term. We will not utilize quotations marks for the remainder of the paper but we will address the problems inherent in this term later in the paper.
2. More information on this project is available in Wallin-Ruschman (2014).
3. A capstone is an upper division course that represents a culminating educational experience in some colleges and universities in the United States.

References

Agness, K. (2015, May 11). Dear universities: There should be no safe spaces from intellectual thought. *Time* Retrieved from http://time .com/3848947/dear-universities-there-should-be-no-safe-spaces-from -intellectual-thought/

Armstrong, E. A. (2002). *Forging gay identities: Organizing sexuality in San Francisco, 1950-1994*. Chicago, IL, USA: University of Chicago Press.

Collins, P. (1999). *Black feminist thought knowledge, consciousness, and the politics of empowerment* (2nd ed.). New York, NY, USA: Routledge.

Ferree, M. M., & Hess, B. B. (2000). *Controversy and coalition: The new feminist movement across three decades of change*. New York, NY, USA: Routledge.

Gamson, W. A. (1991). Commitment and agency in social movement. *Sociological Forum, 6*(1), 27-50. doi:10.1007/BF01112726

Gilligan, C., Spencer, R., Weinberg, M. K., & Bertsch, T. (2003). On the listening guide: A voice-centered relational method. In S. N. Hesse-

Biber & P. Leavy (Eds.), *Emergent methods in social research* (pp. 253-271). Thousand Oaks, CA, USA: SAGE.

Hardt, E. (2013). *In transition: The politics of place-based, prefigurative social movements* (Doctoral dissertation). Retrieved from http://scholarworks.umass.edu/open_access_dissertations/744

Haaken, J., Wallin-Ruschman, J., & Patange, S. (2012). Global hip-hop identities: Black youth, psychoanalytic action research, and the Moving to the Beat project. *Journal of Community & Applied Social Psychology*, 22(1), 63-74. doi:10.1002/casp.1097

Maeckelbergh, M. (2011). Doing is believing: Prefiguration as strategic practice in the alterglobalization movement. *Social Movement Studies: Journal of Social, Cultural and Political Protest*, 10, 1-20. doi:10.1080/14742837.2011.545223

Noonan, P. (2015, May 21). The trigger-happy generation: If reading great literature traumatizes you, wait till you get a taste of adult life. *The Wall Street Journal*. Retrieved from http://www.wsj.com/articles/the-trigger-happy-generation-1432245600

Polletta, F. (1999). "Free spaces" in collective action. *Theory and Society*, 28(1), 1-38. doi:10.1023/A:1006941408302

Polletta, F. (2002). *Freedom is an endless meeting*. Chicago, IL, USA: University of Chicago Press.

Tatum, B. D. (2003). *"Why are all the Black kids sitting together in the cafeteria?": And other conversations about race*. New York, NY, USA: Basic Books.

Wallin-Ruschman, J. (2014). *A girl power study: Looking and listening to the role of emotions and relationality in developing critical consciousness* (Doctoral dissertation). Retrieved from http://archives.pdx.edu/ds/psu/12158

Trigger Warnings Create a Comfortable Working Environment for Students

Tony Pollard

Dr. Tony Pollard is the director of the Centre for Battlefield Archaeology and a senior lecturer and professor of conflict history and archaeology at the University of Glasgow in Scotland.

This semester, I'm teaching my history undergraduates about the Falklands War. As I prepared for one recent class, I gathered examples from my own collection of British tabloid newspapers from 1982 as a primary source. I was however concerned about six copies of the Daily Star, which included photos of topless women. Determined not to offend my students or prompt a complaint, my first inclination was to remove the pages, but I did not want to censor content, particularly as some of these images reflected on the jingoistic coverage of the war—showing models sporting a sailor's cap or toting a rifle.

I settled for a trigger warning at the beginning of the session: "If you are going to be upset by images of semi-naked women don't look at the *Daily Star*, pick one of the other papers." Some chose to look at it, some didn't. It was all very light-hearted, and made my previous worries seem unwarranted. But would it have passed so well without the trigger warning? Possibly not. As it was, I had the opportunity to do the right thing and allowed the students to make their own decisions.

We had barely finished flicking through those old newspapers when today's press once again got exercised about that old chestnut: political correctness gone mad. A trigger warning given by one of my colleagues, Gabriel Moshenska, an archaeologist at University College London, was lambasted in articles in the *Daily Mail* and

The Spectator. Like me, he teaches conflict archaeology, which sheds light on human experience through the study of the physical remains of past wars and other forms of conflict. Also like me, he provides a trigger warning before classes with potentially upsetting content, telling students they can step outside if they wish to. He is right to do so.

Mass Graves Are Traumatic

Archaeology is not just about old bones. There are times when skin, hair and fluids are involved, and yes, even old bones can heighten stress levels. I think back to the mass graves of Australian soldiers buried by the Germans at Fromelles in 1916. My team and I located and evaluated them on behalf of the Australian government and although the remains were skeletal they were still upsetting, with many of them exhibiting the trauma caused by a machine gun burst or grenade blast. Even now when I lecture about the project, it's hard not to get a little choked up about those young men who died such brutal deaths.

This doesn't make me or my students a wuss or mean that I need to man up—it makes me a human being and one sensitive enough to deal with the remains of the dead in a professional and respectful manner.

Some of the material I refer to in my classes is disturbing, with images of the dead appearing regularly. Some of it is material that disturbed me when I first encountered it, and it might well disturb my students. Students are a diverse group, and some of them might have suffered domestic abuse, violent attack or trauma in war—and in some of my classes I know that they have. In these cases, such exposure might trigger flash backs or aggravate recently suppressed trauma. It is only common sense to provide these individuals, and those who just can't stomach images of dead bodies in shallow graves, with the option to walk out of the classroom.

As part of the Masters course on conflict archaeology and heritage at Glasgow University we present examples from forensic archaeology, at times using examples from crime scene cases we have worked on, some of them very unpleasant. It would be totally irresponsible for us not to issue a trigger warning before the class—which would allow the student to leave the room and catch up on course content in a manner more comfortable to them. Responses to this material are difficult to gauge and the suggestion that students shouldn't have chosen the subject in the first place fails to accommodate the complex nature of individual responses, which might even fluctuate from one day to another.

Trigger Warnings Have Their Place

For some time now, the British press has been looking aghast at the situation on university campuses in the US, where trigger warnings and safe spaces have become common place. Now that the trend has crossed the pond there is greater urgency and indignation that the dreaded "PC brigade" are being molly-coddled by left-leaning academics.

In some areas there is perhaps cause for concern, and most definitely debate, if it panders to one group over another prompting an air-brushing of history or threatens freedom of expression. For example, Oriel College at the University of Oxford will not remove a statue of the 19th-century imperialist Cecil Rhodes despite pleas from some quarters that it caused upset. British universities have also experienced a wave of no-platforming of speakers likely to cause offence.

But when it comes to teaching courses with graphic and traumatic content involving past atrocities and death, caution is a must. Do these same journalists get so agitated when a film on TV is preceded by a simple warning that it contains scenes of a sexual nature and graphic violence? I suspect not. It is my opinion that a trigger warning is a mutually satisfying arrangement between student and teacher, and I for one hope they are here to stay.

CHAPTER

Should Political Correctness Be Applied to Social Media and the News?

Overview: Sensitive Topics Are Handled Differently over Social Media

Keith Hampton, Lee Rainie, Weixu Lu, Maria Dwyer, Inyoung Shin, and Kristen Purcell

Keith Hampton is a professor at Michigan State University and a Pew Research Center author; Lee Rainie is the director of internet, science, and technology for Pew Research Center; Weixu Lu is a PhD student at Rutgers University; Inyoung Shin is a PhD student at Rutgers University; and Kristen Purcell is the associate director for research at Pew Research Center's Internet Project.

Summary of Findings

A major insight into human behavior from pre-internet era studies of communication is the tendency of people not to speak up about policy issues in public—or among their family, friends, and work colleagues—when they believe their own point of view is not widely shared. This tendency is called the "spiral of silence."[1]

Some social media creators and supporters have hoped that social media platforms like Facebook and Twitter might produce different enough discussion venues that those with minority views might feel freer to express their opinions, thus broadening public discourse and adding new perspectives to everyday discussion of political issues.

We set out to study this by conducting a survey of 1,801 adults.[2] It focused on one important public issue: Edward Snowden's 2013 revelations of widespread government surveillance of Americans' phone and email records. We selected this issue because other surveys by the Pew Research Center at the time we were fielding this poll showed that Americans were divided over whether the NSA contractor's leaks about surveillance were justified and whether the surveillance policy itself was a good or

"Social Media and the 'Spiral of Silence,'" by Keith Hampton, Lee Rainie, Weixu Lu, Maria Dwyer, Inyoung Shin, and Kristen Purcell, Pew Research Center, August 26, 2014. Reprinted by permission.

bad idea. For instance, Pew Research found in one survey that 44% say the release of classified information harms the public interest while 49% said it serves the public interest.

The survey reported in this report sought people's opinions about the Snowden leaks, their willingness to talk about the revelations in various in-person and online settings, and their perceptions of the views of those around them in a variety of online and off-line contexts.

This survey's findings produced several major insights:

- **People were less willing to discuss the Snowden-NSA story in social media than they were in person.** 86% of Americans were willing to have an in-person conversation about the surveillance program, but just 42% of Facebook and Twitter users were willing to post about it on those platforms.
- **Social media did not provide an alternative discussion platform for those who were not willing to discuss the Snowden-NSA story.** Of the 14% of Americans unwilling to discuss the Snowden-NSA story in person with others, only 0.3% were willing to post about it on social media.
- **In both personal settings and online settings, people were more willing to share their views if they thought their audience agreed with them.** For instance, at work, those who felt their coworkers agreed with their opinion were about three times more likely to say they would join a workplace conversation about the Snowden-NSA situation.
- **Previous "spiral of silence" findings as to people's willingness to speak up in various settings also apply to social media users.** Those who use Facebook were more willing to share their views if they thought their followers agreed with them. If a person felt that people in their Facebook network agreed with their opinion about the Snowden-NSA issue, they were about twice as likely to join a discussion on Facebook about this issue.
- **Facebook and Twitter users were also less likely to share their opinions in many face-to-face settings. This was**

especially true if they did not feel that their Facebook friends or Twitter followers agreed with their point of view. For instance, the average Facebook user (someone who uses the site a few times per day) was half as likely as other people to say they would be willing to voice their opinion with friends at a restaurant. If they felt that their online Facebook network agreed with their views on this issue, their willingness to speak out in a face-to-face discussion with friends was higher, although they were still only 0.74 times as likely to voice their opinion as other people.

Overall, the findings indicate that in the Snowden case, social media did not provide new forums for those who might otherwise remain silent to express their opinions and debate issues. Further, if people thought their friends and followers in social media disagreed with them, they were less likely to say they would state their views on the Snowden NSA story online and in other contexts, such as gatherings of friends, neighbors, or co-workers. This suggests a spiral of silence might spill over from online contexts to in-person contexts, though our data cannot definitively demonstrate this causation. It also might mean that the broad awareness social media users have of their networks might make them more hesitant to speak up because they are especially tuned into the opinions of those around them.

A rundown of the key survey findings:

People reported being less willing to discuss the Snowden-NSA story in social media than they were in person— and social media did not provide an alternative outlet for those reluctant to discuss the issues in person.
Fully 86% of Americans reported in the Pew Research survey they were "very" or "somewhat" willing to have a conversation about the government's surveillance program in at least one of the physical settings we queried—at a public meeting, at a family dinner, at a restaurant with friends, or at work. Yet, only 42% of

those who use Facebook or Twitter were willing to discuss these same issues through social media.

Of the 14% of Americans who were not willing to discuss this issue in person, almost none (0.3%) said they were willing to have a conversation about this issue through social media. This challenges the notion that social media spaces might be considered useful venues for people sharing views they would not otherwise express when they are in the physical presence of others.

Not only were social media sites not an alternative forum for discussion, social media users were less willing to share their opinions in face-to-face settings.

We also did statistical modeling allowing us to more fully understand the findings by controlling for such things as gender, age, education levels, race, and marital status—all of which are related to whether people use social media and how they use it. That modeling allowed us to calculate how likely people were to be willing to express their views in these differing settings holding other things constant.[3]

The results of our analyses show that, even holding other factors such as age constant, social media users are less likely than others to say they would join a discussion about the Snowden-NSA revelations.

- The typical Facebook user—someone who logs onto the site a few times per day—is half as likely to be willing to have a discussion about the Snowden-NSA issues at a physical public meeting as a non-Facebook user.
- Similarly, the typical Twitter user—someone who uses the site a few times per day—is 0.24 times less likely to be willing to share their opinions in the workplace as an internet user who does not use Twitter.

In both offline and online settings, people said they were more willing to share their views on the Snowden-NSA revelations if they thought their audience agreed with them. Previous research has shown that when people decide whether to speak out about an issue, they rely on reference groups—friendships and community ties—to weigh their opinion relative to their peers. In the survey, we asked respondents about their sense of whether different groups of people in their lives agreed or disagreed with their positions on the Snowden leaks. There was some notable variance between those who feel they know the views of their peers and those who do not know what others think. Generally, the more socially close people were—e.g. spouses or family members—the more likely it was that the respondents felt their views matched.

We again calculated how likely it was that someone would be willing to share their views in different settings, depending on their sense of whether their audience agreed with them. We found that, in the case of Snowden's revelations about the NSA, it was clear that if people felt their audience supported them, they were more likely to say they would join a conversation:

- At work, those who felt their coworkers agreed with their opinion on the government's surveillance program were 2.92 times more likely to say they would join a conversation on the topic of Snowden-NSA.
- At a family dinner, those who felt that family members agreed with their opinion were 1.90 times more likely to be willing to discuss the Snowden-NSA issue.
- At a restaurant with friends, if their close friends agreed with their opinion people were 1.42 times more likely to be willing to discuss the Snowden-NSA matter.
- On Facebook, if a person felt that people in their Facebook network agreed with their position on that issue, they were 1.91 times more likely to be willing to join a conversation on the topic of Snowden-NSA.

Those who do not feel that their Facebook friends or Twitter followers agree with their opinion are more likely to self-censor their views on the Snowden-NSA story in many circumstances—in social media and in face-to-face encounters.

In this survey on the Snowden-NSA matter, we found that when social media users felt their opinions were not supported online, they were less likely to say they would speak their minds. This was true not only in social media spaces, but also in the physical presence of others.

- The average Facebook user (someone who uses the site a few times per day) was half as likely as other people to say they would be willing to voice their opinion with friends at a restaurant. If they felt that their online Facebook network agreed with their views on this issue, their willingness to speak out in a face-to-face discussion with friends was higher, although they were still only 0.74 times as likely to voice their opinion.
- The typical Twitter user (who uses the site a few times per day) is 0.24 times as likely to share their opinions with colleagues at work as an internet user who does not use Twitter. However, Twitter users who felt that their online Twitter followers shared their opinion were less reserved: They were only 0.66 times less likely to speak up than other internet users.

The survey did not directly explore why people might remain silent if they felt that their opinions were in the minority. The traditional view of the spiral of silence is that people choose not to speak out for fear of isolation. Other Pew Research studies have found that it is common for social media users to be mistaken about their friends' beliefs and to be surprised once they discover their friends' actual views via social media. Thus, it might be the case that people do not want to disclose their minority views for fear of disappointing their friends, getting into fruitless arguments, or losing them entirely. Some people may prefer not to share their views on social media because their posts persist and can be found later—perhaps by prospective employers or others with high status. As to why the absence of agreement on social media platforms spills over into a spiral of silence in physical settings, we speculate that social media users may have witnessed those with minority opinions experiencing ostracism, ridicule or bullying online, and that this might increase the perceived risk of opinion sharing in other settings.

People also say they would speak up, or stay silent, under specific conditions.

In addition to exploring the impact of agreement/disagreement on whether people were willing to discuss the Snowden-NSA revelations, we asked about other factors that might shape whether people would speak out, even if they suspected they held minority views. This survey shows how the social and political climate in which people share opinions depends on several other things:

- **Their confidence in how much they know.** Those who felt they knew a lot about the issues were more likely than others to say they would join conversations.
- **The intensity of their opinions.** Those who said they had strong feelings about the Snowden-NSA matter were more willing than those with less intense feelings to talk about the subject.
- **Their level of interest.** Those who said they were very interested in the Snowden-NSA story were more likely than those who were not as interested to express their opinions.

People's use of social media did little to increase their access to information about the Snowden-NSA revelations.

We asked respondents where they were getting information about the debates swirling around the Snowden revelations, and found that social media was not a common source of news for most Americans. Traditional broadcast news sources were by far the most common sources. In contrast, social media sources like

Facebook and Twitter were the least commonly identified sources for news on this issue.

- 58% of all adults got at least some information on the topic of Snowden-NSA from TV or radio.
- 34% got at least some information from online sources other than social media.[4]
- 31% got at least some information from friends and family.
- 19% got at least some information from a print newspaper.
- 15% got at least some information while on Facebook.
- 3% got at least some information from Twitter.

There are limits to what this snapshot can tell us about how social media use is related to the ways Americans discuss important political issues. This study focuses on one specific public affairs issue that was of interest to most Americans: the Snowden-NSA revelations. It is not an exhaustive review of all public policy issues and the way they are discussed in social media.

The context of the Snowden-NSA story may also have made it somewhat different from other kinds of public debates. At the time of this study, the material leaked by Edward Snowden related to NSA monitoring of communications dealt specifically with "meta-data" collected on people's phone and internet communications. For a phone call, the meta-data collected by the NSA was described as including the duration of the call, when it happened, the numbers the call was between, but not a recording of the call. For email, meta-data would have included the sender and recipient's email addresses and when it was sent, but not the subject or text of the email.

Additional information leaked by Snowden after our study was completed suggests that Western intelligence agencies monitored and manipulated the content of online discussions and the NSA recorded the content of foreign phone calls. In reaction to these additional revelations, people may have adjusted their use of social media and their willingness to discuss a range of topics, including public issues such as government surveillance. However, given the limited extent of the information leaked by Snowden at the time the survey was fielded, it seems unlikely that the average American had extensively altered their willingness to discuss political issues. Future research may provide insight into whether Americans have become more or less willing to discuss specific issues on-and offline as a result of government surveillance programs. While this study focused on the Snowden-NSA revelations, we suspect that Americans use social media in similar ways to discuss and get news about other political issues.

About This Report

An informed citizenry depends on people's exposure to information on important political issues and on their willingness to discuss these issues with those around them. The rise of social media, such as Facebook and Twitter, has introduced new spaces where political discussion and debate can take place. This report explores the degree to which social media affects a long-established human attribute—that those who think they hold minority opinions often self-censor, failing to speak out for fear of ostracism or ridicule. It is called the "spiral of silence."

This report is a collaborative effort based on the input and analysis of the following individuals:[5]

Keith N. Hampton, Associate Professor, Rutgers University
Lee Rainie, Director, Internet Project
Weixu Lu, PhD student, Rutgers University
Maria Dwyer, PhD student, Rutgers University
Inyoung Shin, PhD student, Rutgers University
Kristen Purcell, Associate Director for Research, Internet Project

About This Survey

This report contains findings from a nationally representative survey of 1,801 American adults (ages 18+) conducted by the Pew Research Center and fielded August 7-September 16, 2013 by Princeton Research Associates International. It was conducted in English and Spanish on landline (N=901) and cell phones

(N=900). The margin of error for the full sample is plus or minus 2.6 percentage points. Some 1,076 respondents are users of social networking sites and the margin of error for that subgroup is plus or minus 3.3 percentage points.

Endnotes

1. Noelle-Neumann, E. (1974). "The Spiral of Silence A Theory of Public Opinion." Journal of Communication 24(2): 43-51.

2. The survey was conducted between August 7-September 16, 2013 and has a margin of error of plus or minus 2.6 percentage points for the full sample.

3. We report the odds based on a logistic regression. The outcome of a logistic regression tells us the probability that a person will do something based on the relationship to a series of predictor variables. For example, if half of the people in our sample are willing to speak out at a public meeting, but half are not, the probability of doing something is 50%., i.e., a 50-50 percent chance, the odds are equal, 1 to 1. The odds are a ratio of the probability that a person will do something over the probability that they will not. Let's say, hypothetically, that 80% of the people in our sample were willing to speak with family about an issue, this means that 20% were not. The odds that they would speak out are .8/.2 = 4. That is to say, the odds that someone would speak with family are 4 to 1, or are 4 times higher, or are 4 times more likely to occur. Throughout this report, we use that language.

4. In this survey, 80% of adults said they were internet users, 71% of the internet users are Facebook users, and 18% of internet users are Twitter users.

5. We are grateful to the following individuals for their comments and advice as we developed this work: Pablo Boczkowski (Northwestrn University), William Eveland (The Ohio State University), and Rima Wilkes (University of British Columbia).

Anti-PC Sentiment Is a Detriment to Our Culture

Lance Selfa

Lance Selfa is a writer whose works include the book Democrats: A Critical History.

I t's become a ritual by now. As soon as news of a campus protest against racism or sexism emerges, you can count on the media filling up with outraged commentaries against "political correctness" run amok.

Rather than address the substance of the protests themselves, well-paid pundits fulminate against "coddled" students who can't accept a little real-world unpleasantness and who want to police everyone else's "free speech."

Of course, you can always count on the likes of Bill O'Reilly and his cohorts at Fox News to denounce this creeping "totalitarianism" on campus. But the media now have their go-to liberals like Jonathan Chait or Michelle Goldberg to wag their fingers at today's protesters.

The rhetoric against "political correctness" has found its way into the Republican primaries, with racists like Donald Trump wearing it as a badge of honor. Trump calls Mexican immigrants rapists and drug dealers and says the government should register Muslims in a database. And when anyone objects, Trump congratulates himself for his courage to dish out insults at oppressed people rather than cave to the conventions of "political correctness."

When ABC News' George Stephanopolous confronted Trump with the fact that there was no evidence for his claim that hundreds of people in New Jersey celebrated the September 11 attacks, Trump responded: "I know it might not be politically correct for you

"The crusade against 'political correctness,'" by Lance Selfa, SocialistWorker.org, December 8, 2015. Reprinted by permission.

to talk about it, but there were people cheering as that building came down."

Given how pervasive these set-piece confrontations over "political correctness" are, it's easy to forget that this wasn't always the lens through which the media viewed campus protest. In fact, the campaign against "political correctness" (PC) was established as a conscious effort on the part of right-wing ideologues in the late 1980s and early 1990s.

This campaign hit a high point in May 1991 when President George H.W. Bush, addressing the University of Michigan commencement, warned that "political extremists roam the land, abusing the privilege of free speech, setting citizens against one another on the basis of their class or race." As Bush continued:

> The notion of political correctness has ignited controversy across the land. Although the movement arises from a laudable desire to sweep away the debris of racism and sexism and hatred, it replaces old prejudices with new ones. It declares certain topics off-limits, certain expressions off-limits, even certain gestures off-limits.

By today's Trumpian standards, Bush's speech seems almost genteel. But there was nothing genteel about the campaign that pushed the anti-PC crusade onto the president's agenda.

In late 1990 and early 1991, cover stories like "The P.C. Front," "The Victims' Revolution," "The Storm Over the University," and "Thought Police" appeared in *Time, Atlantic, Newsweek, The New York Review of Books, The New Republic* and a host of other publications. According to these reports, U.S. campuses had been overrun by PC "thought police," who were conducting a witch hunt against people with whom they disagreed: conservative students, right-wing lecturers or professors who upheld the "canon" of Western literature and thought.

This was before the widespread use of the Internet, 24-hour cable news shows and even before Fox News, but the rhetoric around PC escalated rapidly anyway. Conservative columnist George Will penned a tribute to Lynne Cheney, then chair of the

National Endowment for the Humanities, who played the role of culture warrior for "traditional values":

> Lynne Cheney is secretary of domestic defense. The foreign adversaries her husband, Dick, must keep at bay are less dangerous, in the long run, than the domestic forces with which she must deal. Those forces are fighting against the conservation of the common culture that is the nation's social cement.

Before the anti-PC crusade, the term "political correctness" had been part of the jargon of the left. It took on a number of meanings, from assuming an "orthodox" position on all political questions, to conforming one's personal and interpersonal behavior to one's political ideals.

Max Elbaum's description of the late 1960s-early 1970s Maoist-influenced "new communist movement" gives a feel for the time:

> Their high level of commitment made movement cadre willing to engage in self-criticism, not only to learn better organizing skills but to unlearn conduct that reflected narrow individualism or race, class or (less frequently) gender privilege. Self-transformation was seen as an integral, if subordinate, aspect of social transformation.

New York Times columnist William Safire, the conservative who for years wrote a column on English language usage, cited Black feminist Toni Cade Bambara, who wrote in 1970's *The Black Woman: An Anthology* that "a man cannot be politically correct and a [male] chauvinist, too."

Later, as the New Left movements declined, the term took on a more ironic tone, as activists poked fun at what they perceived as their comrades' overly zealous or dogmatic stances or wondered if it was "politically correct" to make certain career or personal decisions.

Whatever its exact origin or shortcomings, "political correctness" emerged from a milieu of people and groups dedicated to changing the world and fighting oppression. The term was definitely not used, as it is today, to excuse racist or sexist behavior.

Until the mainstream media began to promote the anti-PC crusade, it generally had been the concern of right-wing ideologues like University of Chicago philosopher Allan Bloom. One of the opening shots of the PC war, Bloom's 1987 best seller *The Closing of the American Mind* blamed 1960s radical movements for undermining the quality of scholarship and university life.

Then in 1989, William Bennett, the Reagan administration's former Education Secretary and the Bush Administration's "drug czar," gave Bloom's ideas concrete expression when he attacked Stanford University for revising its core reading list for freshmen.

Suddenly, right-wing academics and pundits were vying with one another to condemn "multiculturalism" and to report tales of anti-imperialist and anti-European bias on campus.

A steady stream of books and articles, funded by conservative think tanks such as the Olin Foundation, the American Enterprise Institute and the Scaife Foundation, pounded away at these themes. One of these, Roger Kimball's 1990 *Tenured Radicals*, proclaimed, "What we have witnessed is nothing less than the occupation of the center by a new academic establishment, the establishment of tenured radicals."

Of course, the lurid tales of PC tyranny and charges of radicalism were figments of the PC bashers' imaginations.

In 1987, the American Council on Education noted a 20-year upward trend of undergraduates majoring in business—hardly the work of Marxist radicals! The 1990 Higher Education Research Institute survey found that only about 5 percent of faculty members identified themselves as "far left," compared to the 18 percent who identified themselves as conservative. And a 1992 Modern Language Association study noted that in the previous decade, only four college English departments had dropped courses in Shakespeare—compared to 18 that eliminated altogether courses in Black or ethnic literature.

In one of his more honest moments, conservative pundit John Podhoretz, who cut his teeth with the conservative newspaper at the University of Chicago, granted that universities became more conservative in the 1980s. "There's a fundamental redirection going on," Podhoretz said in 1985. "The world is a more hospitable place for conservative ideology today in a way it certainly wasn't in the 1970s. My friends and I no longer have to consider ourselves an embattled minority."

None of this really mattered to the anti-PC crusaders. They were after bigger targets. In particular, they wanted to roll back the gains of the 1960s and 1970s movements: affirmative action programs, open admissions policies, abortion rights and LGBT rights. The anti-PC crusade became an all-purpose front behind which the right wing attacked any opinion that got in the way of its attempt to turn back the clock.

Dinesh D'Souza made this clear in his 1991 *Illiberal Education*, where he linked multiculturalism to affirmative action and women's and minority studies programs. All of these were part of a "victim's revolution," he argued, that produced a "grievance industry" concocting allegations of racism and discrimination to hide the inability of women and minorities to keep up with college-level work.

D'Souza became the star of the anti-PC crusade. Unlike the cranky old white men like Bennett and Bloom, D'Souza was young—he turned 30 when *Illiberal Education* debuted—and a person of color. He made a name for himself earlier in conservative circles as a collegiate editor for the right-wing *Dartmouth Review* in the 1980s and as a "domestic policy adviser" to the Reagan White House.

D'Souza was the product of a "farm system" of young conservatives that right-wing foundations created during the 1980s.

When the Reagan era began in 1981, a network of conservative student publications and organizations appeared on major campuses around the country. Sustained by grants and technical support from the Institute for Educational Affairs and other conservative foundations, the number of those publications hit 50 by 1989. Support from wealthy conservatives put young conservatives in contact with the larger orbit of conservative foundations, advertisers and supporters—which reached as high as the White House itself.

The right-wing journalists "sit around some pretty significant dinner tables," said Dartmouth College's public affairs director at the time. "There are any number of U.S. senators and congressmen they can call and get their calls returned." Many of these conservative "activists" made an easy transition from campus to positions at conservative Washington think tanks, congressional and White House staffs, and, later, the conservative media.

The most notorious of the right-wing campus rags was D'Souza's *Dartmouth Review*, founded in 1980.

During D'Souza's tenure as editor from 1981 to 1983, the *Review* printed such quips as "genocide means never having to say you're sorry" and advertised a story on the Ku Klux Klan with a staged picture of a Black man hanging from a tree. In 1981, the *Review* published an article by D'Souza outing officers of the Dartmouth Gay Students Association and printed excerpts from confidential personal letters of GSA members. D'Souza's articles were based on documents stolen from GSA files.

Even after D'Souza had decamped to Washington to write a biography of far-right Rev. Jerry Falwell, the *Review* kept up its antics. In 1986, people associated with the paper destroyed an anti-apartheid shantytown with baseball bats and sledgehammers. Two years later, two *Review* staffers physically attacked one of the two Black professors on the Dartmouth campus.

The *Dartmouth Review*'s provocations were the most extreme of the 1980s campus right, but they weren't the only ones. In 1984, a *Northwestern Review* staffer, on a field trip with the counterrevolutionary forces fighting the left-wing Nicaraguan government, published gruesome pictures of a contra execution of a "communist."

In 1990, University of Iowa *Campus Review* editor Jeffrey Renander led a counterdemonstration to the Iowa City LGBT pride parade. Mocking the AIDS Quilt, Renander and his cohorts carried a "gerbil quilt" that purported to memorialize gerbils "[that] die every year" from "certain sexual practices."

Those outrages were just a few examples of the sort of filth that so-called conservative "activists" and "journalists," using corporate and alumni money, brought to U.S. campuses. The whole aim of the operation was to shift the general political climate to the right, and to make racism, sexism and anti-gay prejudice "respectable" on campus.

The attack on PC was the work of ideologically committed conservatives who worked through networks like IEA. It was not the work of disinterested scholars, but of a small core of right-wing ideologues. With corporate money and the mass media at their disposal, the PC bashers were no embattled minority. They were well-paid hired guns for those who hold power in Washington and Corporate America.

Looking back over this history in light of recent controversies on campus, it becomes clear just how successful the anti-PC crusade was. Not only does the "political correctness" canard emerge just about every time a campus mobilizes against racism or sexism, but now liberals like Chait try to beat conservatives into print.

Plenty of prospects from the 1980s conservative collegiate farm system have made it to the majors. They aren't a persecuted minority, but fixtures in the conservative opinion establishment.

Laura Ingraham, one of D'Souza's partners in crime at Dartmouth, is a conservative media star, with a national radio show and a slot on Fox. Podhoretz is the editor of Commentary and a columnist for the *New York Daily News*. Ann Coulter, editor of the *Cornell Review* in the mid-1980s, is a best-selling author known for her steady patter of consciously offensive statements against Blacks, immigrants, Muslims, liberals and other targets of conservatives.

One-time *Harvard Salient* editor Ross Douthat speaks out against attacks on the conservatives' free speech from his bunker in the *New York Times* editorial page. Peter Thiel, first editor of the *Stanford Review*, is a libertarian billionaire who founded PayPal.

Of all of them, D'Souza has probably had the worst run of bad luck. After re-grabbing the spotlight with his ridiculous 2010 book *The Roots of Obama's Rage* and a 2012 documentary film based on it, he pled guilty in 2012 to making illegal contributions to a U.S. Senate campaign. He's now on probation after serving eight months in a halfway house in San Diego.

More seriously, the bitter fruit of the early 1990s ideological campaign against political correctness can be seen in its more tangible, material results.

After a series of Supreme Court decisions and referendum results, affirmative action on U.S. campuses is hanging by a thread. Cases of sexual assault on campus are still met with victim-blaming and bureaucratic incompetence.

And as much as conservatives prattle on about attacks on free speech, the real attacks on campus free speech have come from their side. Witness the outlawing of Chicano studies in Arizona or the "Palestine exception" to on-campus debate about Israel and Palestine.

In the neoliberal era, higher education has become increasingly transformed into an expensive commodity, sustained by underpaid and precarious labor and onerous levels of student debt. It's a system that's more attuned to "educating for austerity" than for encouraging critical thought about society or the economy.

That's just fine with the purveyors of the line about the "closing of the American mind."

A PC Environment Contributes to Creativity and Openness

Gene Demby

Gene Demby is lead blogger for NPR's Code Switch team. He was previously managing editor of Huffington Post's BlackVoices *and has held various positions at the* New York Times.

By now, you've surely seen Jonathan Chait's sprawling takedown of what he describes as a dangerous resurgence of political correctness in the 21st century. In his telling, a "PC culture" that flourished on college campuses in the '90s is back, stronger than ever thanks to Twitter and social media, and it's been crippling political discourse—and maybe even democracy itself.

There have been elated cosigns. There has been sharp pushback.

I'm not the first to point out that Chait offers little in the way of hard evidence to back up his warnings. He gives a lot of weight to comments lifted from a Facebook page and an incident in which a feminist studies professor shoved a protester. He also notes the complaints lodged by a few high-profile and well-connected authors that Change.org petitions, Twitter hashtags and other forms of social media pushback have made them gun-shy about opinionating online.

But when we're worrying over the future of human communication and the future of democracy—anecdotes and isolated incidents are only part of the conversation. They aren't enough on their own. And since Chait doesn't present research on how political correctness may or may not affect the way people exchange ideas, I decided to go looking for it.

Michelle Duguid, a professor of organizational behavior at Washington University in St. Louis, has co-authored one such study, inspired by an offhand debate with some colleagues over whether political correctness hurts or helps productivity. Unlike the rest of us, Duguid and her peers had the means to empirically test their positions. The result is a study published last year by Cornell University.

Here's how the study worked: The researchers asked hundreds of college students to brainstorm new business ideas for an empty restaurant space on campus. But first, they separated the students into groups and instructed some of the groups to discuss an instance of political correctness they'd heard or personally experienced. They did this to effectively put the notion of political correctness into their collective heads and impose what they call a "PC norm" on the group as a whole. (You can read the study for the science behind this.) Other groups got no such instruction.

The researchers found that groups that had both men and women and had been exposed to the PC norm went on to generate more ideas—and more novel ideas—for how to use the vacant lot than the mixed-gender groups that hadn't discussed political correctness. (The ideas were graded for "novelty" by an independent panel, based on how much an idea diverged from the rest.)

The researchers' takeaway: By imposing a PC environment, they had made it easier for men and women to speak their minds in mixed company. They had "reduced the uncertainty" that can come with interacting with someone from the opposite sex.

"Our work challenges the widespread assumption that true creativity requires a kind of anarchy in which people are permitted to speak their minds, whatever the consequence," Jack Goncalo, the study's lead author, has said.

"The big part of it that we found is that you should act a certain way [in any group setting] and there are sanctions if you don't act in that way," Duguid told me.

All groups have implied norms—maybe around political correctness, say, but also around things like how to dress or speak or pray—and not following those rules might earn furious side-eyes if not straight-up ostracism.

What's more, the researchers believe political correctness could have "similar, and perhaps even stronger effects" in groups with other kinds of diversity, like race, "which can heighten uncertainty and trigger anxiety."

"Until the uncertainty caused by demographic differences can be overcome within diverse groups," they conclude, "the effort to be PC can be justified not merely on moral grounds, but also by the practical and potentially profitable consequences of facilitating the exchange of creative ideas."

That is to say, it's a lot easier for people in mixed company—i.e., everywhere, increasingly—to come up with great ideas together with the benefit of a social blueprint.

Duguid warned me that my hunt for more peer-reviewed research on the subject of political correctness and group dynamics would be short. She called the field "barren," and indeed her study is the only one I've found so far that looks squarely at political correctness and speech.

And to be sure, this study measured creativity in a workplace-like setting, while Chait's major concern is the marketplace of ideas. He's not necessarily suggesting that PC culture is bad for business. It's liberal discourse that's under assault, he warns, and political correctness threatens to take the very foundations of democracy down with it.

"Politics in a democracy is still based on getting people to agree with you, not making them afraid to disagree," Chait writes.

But I would argue that the Cornell study has a place in this conversation. It's measuring people's abilities to communicate with each other in productive ways, as well as the ways imposing constraints on speech helps or hurts that effort. It's not that big a jump to apply implications for workplace performance to the realm of political effectiveness.

Chait's certainly right about one thing: The culture wars play out differently in the age of social media. But the rancor we see on Twitter may not be an indication that political correctness is making it harder to talk to each other. It may be simply be a byproduct of where the debate is taking place. The rules of engagement on social media platforms are in their infancy; after all, Twitter only introduced a "report abuse" button in 2013. And Twitter, famously, magnifies voices, meaning a few dedicated, sufficiently loud dissenters in a conversation can sometimes feel like an angry, critical mass. It's much harder to encourage—or trick— the thousands of people fighting across a given Twitter hashtag into norms of politeness than a controlled group of study participants.

It's just one study, but we know that political correctness is a measurable thing. Future studies might even bear out Chait's thesis. But marshaling a whole bunch of compelling anecdotes about the pernicious effects of political correctness isn't enough to make Chait's point true.

Political Correctness Is Unnecessary and Manipulative

Luis R. Miranda

Luis R. Miranda is the founder and editor of the Real Agenda News.

olitical correctness is key in centralizing power. That is
why more and more people, who are purportedly liberal
or progressive, are all out to curve people's choice of words and
even thoughts.

The growing number of people who think that individuals'
speech should be regulated by the government to avoid politically
incorrect statements are persons who have been hiding under
the shadows for a long time as victims of the hatred they feel for
their own lives.

People who feel entitled to restrain someone else's speech are
what I have come to call the "perpetually offended." Scholars and
academics who analyze the current move towards intellectual
slavery as well as people who are well-aware about the agenda
behind enforcing politically correct speech have found very
insightful information about the "thought police."

The real agenda behind politically correct speech and
intolerance towards a diversity of ideas is that political correctness
is a manipulative tool for centralizing power. Just as that that who
counts the votes is more important than those who vote, and just
as those who control food can control a population; controlling
speech enables diversity-of-thought haters to take over people's
mental abilities.

"The left is definitely using these mass manipulation tactics,"
says Stella Morabito, a former intelligence analyst. She says that
conservatives have no clue about the propaganda manipulation

"Political Correctness: The World Of The Perpetually Offended," by Luis R. Miranda, Novomag theme, February 18, 2016 (http://real-agenda.com/the-world-of-the-perpetually-offended/). Reprinted by permission of Luis R. Miranda.

tactics and that most people in the left aren't even knowledgeable enough to understand it. They just go along with the flow.

According to Morabito, mass ignorance is key in bringing about the type of society we live in and the kind of environment the Elite has planned for us all. She says that the very human fear of being rejected is one of the pillars of the current move to divide social groups that would otherwise make strong links among individuals.

In other words, people, who for a long time have felt left out, are the most likely to open their ears and join so-called liberal movements. Unsuspecting supporters of Feminism, LGBT, Gender Equality and other left-wing movements are included in the group of potential victims.

Recently, Thierry Meyssan explained how companies that are in the business of setting up campaigns and movements work in favor of a candidate or an idea to make it mainstream.

Separating society into small groups and making those groups go after each other is paramount if the Elite is to be successful in destroying human identity. Language manipulation through the imposition of a veil of semantic fog has become a powerful tool in turning individuals into self-censoring, mindless and easily controllable beings.

If we revisit the example of the "quick public opinion shift" on same-sex marriage—which was basically an implausible idea 15 years ago—we might ask: why did the activist push for it became so fast and furious? Couldn't the idea withstand real public discourse and stand on its own merits without extreme public shaming of anyone who had doubts? Couldn't it have come about through the legislative process without an activist judge overturning the referendum results of an entire state? Or Supreme Court justices claiming that those opposed were filled with "animus"?

The effective capture of society is done via the most important communication outlets, including the media, Hollywood, pop culture, academia, religion, and more recently, the family. "If you push an agenda to centralize power, you need mass ignorance and effective propaganda," Morabito explains.

The Elite's agenda to centralize power and control is brought upon society in disguise, hidden behind messages of fairness, equality and anyone who dares speak their mind against the brainwashing movement is immediately accused of driving homophobic speech, racism, anti-Semitism, of being a womanizer, a holocaust denier, a "flat earther" and so on.

"Opinion cascades, particularly on ideas that seem implausible— rely on a great deal of propaganda and agitation, through political correctness. They are very fragile things. The survival of such opinion cascades requires a lot of tweaking and teasing and discipline and balancing acts by those pushing them, including activists, politicians, celebrities, academics, media moguls." That is precisely how the masses of the perpetually offended get mobilized. In simple terms, the Elite gives the naked Emperor a new set of clothes that only the brainwashed are able to see. In reality, though, the Emperor is naked. "It's all about conditioning," says Morabito.

When propaganda alone does not work, the Elite resources to PsyOps. Psychological Operations are far more complex than propaganda, which is aimed only at deforming the perception of reality. This tactic is often used to convince people who have resisted the propaganda and to reinforce the thoughts of those who are already in the bag.

Companies like SCL, whose business is to profile human drones and zombies who feel left out, offer their services which include "using behavioural techniques in order to fabricate a political party which would sweep its client to power." Psychologists in these company and others "define the profile type of the sincere and manipulable militant." Later, data is collected, usually by paying off companies like Amazon to obtain data from target populations. An analysis is conducted to find out who best fits the profile. Based on this information, the company designs a message that will convince people to support their idea or personality.

"Through propaganda and agitation, you get behavior modification on a mass scale. Yesterday it was same sex marriage. Today it is transgenderism. Tomorrow? It could be absolutely anything at all."

The techniques used to manipulate masses of people come directly from academia, where specific terms are employed to name mass manipulation tactics. "Availability cascade" is an academic term that basically has to do with manufacturing public opinion approval for a policy of some sort. "Any kind of policy at all," explains Morabito.

Brainwashing the masses is as easy as injecting a new idea into public discourse, to turn it available to the target masses. Fake populism is one of the best tools to manipulate the public, which is why politicians have attempted to master populism for a long time. The goal is to "saturate the media with praises for the idea, and add just the right celebrity endorsements," says Morabito. We saw this tactic during Super Bowl 50's halftime show, where performers used explicit visual tools to send a message to the dissatisfied masses of people who were tuning into the broadcast.

The dangers of falling for the political correctness gimmick is that there is no way back. Once people fall in the deep hole of thought control, there is little to do to bring them back. "We need far more conversations about how political correctness— i.e., coercive thought reform—undermines our ability to think independently," warns Morabito. She agrees with the fact that once people's ability to think freely is gone, they become ideal subjects of manipulation. "On a mass scale, this is very bad for any society."

The question is, how do we prevent ourselves and other people who live around us from being manipulated? How can we build a shield of protection against coercive thought reform? The answer is, by learning more about it, by learning how to identify it and how to reject it. Once we are able to create a shield, it is possible to go out and help others. Put it simply, it is necessary to hack-proof your mind.

Publishers and News Media Pander to Bias and Ignorance

Walter Brasch

Walter Brasch was a social issues journalist who authored several books, including Fracking America *and* Before the First Snow.

The Texas board of education didn't find anything wrong with a world geography textbook that said slaves from Africa were workers, but that immigrants from northern Europe were indentured servants.

This is the same school board that five years ago demanded that textbooks emphasize that slavery was only a side issue to the cause of the civil war, and that Republican achievements be emphasized in political science and civics textbooks.

For good measure, the officials also wanted a "fair and balanced" look at evolution versus intelligent design or creationism, and that global warming is only a theory, overlooking substantial and significant scientific evidence.

Because Texas adopts textbooks for the entire state, and there is minimal local choice, publishers tend to publish what Texas wants. The geography book had a 100,000 sale in Texas alone. However, McGraw-Hill, under a firestorm of protest from educators and parents, is modifying the text—African slaves will no longer be "workers" but slaves in the next printing.

Publishers in America, trying to reap the widest possible financial benefit by not offending anyone, especially school boards, often force authors to overlook significant historical and social trends. For more than a century, books which targeted buyers in the North consistently overlooked or minimized Southern views about the Civil War; other books, which targeted a Southern readership,

"Today's Media: Often Pandering to Bias and Ignorance," by Walter Brasch, The Moderate Voice. Reprinted by permission.

discussed the War of Northern Aggression or the War Between the States.

Almost all media overlooked significant issues about slavery, the genocide against Native Americans, the real reasons for the Mexican-American War, the seizure of personal property and subsequent incarceration of Japanese-American citizens during World War II, the reasons why the United States went to war in Vietnam, the first Gulf War and, more recent, the wars in Iraq and Afghanistan. Textbook publishers, choosing profits over truth, often glossed over, or completely ignored until years or decades later, the major social movements, including the civil rights, anti-war and peace movements of the 1960s and the emerging environmental movement of the 1970s. It was the underground and alternative press that presented the truth that the establishment press under-reported or refused to acknowledge, timidly accepting the "official sources."

Textbook publishers aren't the only problem. The news media have ignored or downplayed mass protests against the wars, whether Vietnam or Iraq. They have ignored or downplayed mass protests against fracking. And, during this election year, all media have decided which candidates should get the most news coverage. There are several excellent Republican presidential candidates, but the media like the pompous and boisterous Donald Trump; he gives a good show. On the Democratic side, Hillary Clinton gets the most coverage of the three major candidates. Analysis of network air time by the Tyndall Reports shows that ABC-TV's "World News Tonight" during the past year gave Donald Trump 81 minutes of air; it gave Sen. Bernie Sanders less than a minute, although Sanders is drawing even larger crowds than Trump. It's no different with CBS and NBC television coverage. Total broadcast network time for Trump, according to Tyndall's data, is 234 minutes; for Sanders, it's about 10 minutes. The problem, of course, is editorializing by omission.

At one time, the media led the nation in unveiling social injustice and other major problems. Although they had their defects and biases, the nation's media understood they were the system that helped assure a free and unencumbered forum for debate about major issues. More important, they also understood that their role wasn't to perpetuate fraud and lies, but to seek out and present the truth. Seemingly in conflict—present all views vs. present the facts and the truth—the media also understood that newsprint and airtime should not be wasted upon being a megaphone for ignorance. Now, their role is to follow, while pandering to the entertainment value of social and political issues and giving cursory glances at the news value. It's not what the Founding Fathers believed and, certainly, not what they wanted. But it is, in the 21st century, the media's vain attempt to restore profits.

Chapter 4

Has PC Culture
Gone Too Far?

Overview: The Debate Over Political Correctness Continues

Chris Green

Chris Green is Scotland editor at the Independent *and the* Independent on Sunday.

To most people, it might seem innocuous enough: an email from a lecturer at Yale University suggesting that her students should try not to be offended if they saw one of their peers wearing a culturally insensitive Halloween costume. "Is there no room any more for a child or young person to be a little bit obnoxious … a little bit inappropriate or provocative or, yes, offensive?" she asked.

But the message from Erika Christakis, which had been designed to pacify rather than enrage, blew up in her face. She and her husband Nicholas, who are masters at Yale's Silliman College and live among the students, are now facing calls to resign from their positions, move out of their home and leave the university for good. Some students have even threatened to leave the college if they refuse.

Several American commentators have expressed their bewilderment at how an apparently mild email encouraging students to think, debate and not to overreact could be enough to provoke a hate mob. The incident has reignited the debate over whether today's students are being "coddled" and universities turned into places where they are constantly shielded from words and ideas that might make them uncomfortable.

It is not a debate confined to the United States. In the UK similar concerns were raised last month, when Germaine Greer was forced to pull out of a lecture at Cardiff University after students launched

"Political correctness: Debate over whether it has gone too far rages at universities from Cambridge to Yale," by Chris Green, Independent.co.uk, November 15, 2015. Reprinted by permission.

a petition accusing her of holding "misogynistic views" towards trans women and calling on her to be barred from speaking.

Over the summer, students at the University of Oxford's Oriel College called for the removal of a statue of Cecil Rhodes, the founder of the South African territory of Rhodesia. The group claimed it was a monument to racism and colonialism, with one member telling reporters: "There's a violence to having to walk past the statue every day on the way to your lectures."

In the US, students have also requested that so-called "trigger warnings" be included on the front covers of classic works of literature, in case people who have had distressing experiences of sexual violence, racism or other traumas are caught off-guard and find themselves reliving the past.

Books named by American students at various universities as potentially requiring trigger warnings were said to include *Things Fall Apart* by Chinua Achebe, *The Great Gatsby* by F Scott Fitzgerald, *Mrs Dalloway* by Virginia Woolf and Shakespeare's *The Merchant of Venice*. In the UK, the idea has been dismissed by lecturers and academics including John Mullan, professor of English at University College London, who said last year: "You might as well put a label on English literature saying: 'Warning— bad stuff happens here.'"

This apparent rise in the general stifling of debate on American campuses—and the danger that the phenomenon poses to the future of the students passing through today's universities—was recently discussed at length in an influential essay in The Atlantic magazine by Greg Lukianoff and Jonathan Haidt. It is entitled: "The Coddling of the American Mind."

Arguing that the modern rush to take offence should be described as "vindictive protectiveness" and should not be confused with the hackneyed phrase "political correctness," the authors say it is creating a culture in which "everyone must think twice before speaking up, lest they face charges of insensitivity, aggression, or worse."

They continue: "What exactly are students learning when they spend four years or more in a community that polices unintentional slights, places warning labels on works of classic literature, and in many other ways conveys the sense that words can be forms of violence that require strict control by campus authorities?"

The fear of offence is felt keenly by the people who run universities, as the incident involving Ms Christakis at Yale shows. Her email was written in response to a campus-wide message circulated by the university's Intercultural Affairs Committee which urged students planning on dressing up for Halloween to do so sensitively. The email, signed off by no fewer than 13 Yale administrative staff, told students to ask themselves a series of questions before donning their costume. They included: "Is the humour based on 'making fun' of real people, human traits or cultures? Does it further misinformation or historical and cultural inaccuracies? Does this costume mock or belittle someone's deeply held faith tradition?"

Ironically, some students at Yale objected that this initial email had been too heavy-handed, provoking Ms Christakis's contribution and the furore that followed. In today's universities, it seems, it is increasingly difficult to please anyone.

Glossary key terms in the free speech debate

The debate around the "new political correctness" on university campuses in the US and the UK involves many terms that may be unfamiliar to readers. Here are some of the buzzwords used by those on both sides of the argument:

Safe spaces

Places intended to be free from discrimination, harassment and hate speech against any underprivileged groups, such as women, LGBT people and ethnic minorities. A protected area where the usual discrimination and prejudices that these groups might encounter in everyday life doesn't exist. People can be removed from the "safe space" if their disagreeable views threaten this.

Trigger warnings
Sometimes called "content notes," a warning at the top of an article or front of a book that lets people know of distressing content such as rape, violence or racism.

Microaggressions
Minor slights or snubs that are usually unintended but can be perceived by the recipient as evidence of underlying prejudicial assumptions. For example, asking an Asian student why he "isn't good at math."

No-platforming
Refusing to give a platform to speakers or writers who have previously espoused controversial views—for instance, refusing to let a prominent feminist who doesn't accept that transgender women are women speak at a university.

Vindictive protectiveness
A term used by critics of "the new political correctness" to describe the behaviour of censorious students. They argue that through excessive molly-coddling, the creation of false spaces which don't represent the complexities of the world, and the establishment of environments where anyone who disagrees with the majority view is silenced, young people are failing to build resilience and actually end up damaging their own mental health.

Catastrophising
Believing in the worst-case scenario as a result of trauma in the past—for instance, a person who has experienced domestic violence might believe that when they make a very minor mistake at work, their boss will fire them. Free speech campaigners have accused some students who take offence at microaggressions of catastrophising.

Intersectionality

The idea that all prejudices intersect, rather than stand on their own. For instance, to examine a person's experience of discrimination in society, we shouldn't just focus on the fact that they are black, but also that they are female and working class.

Cisgender

A person whose gender and biological sex align; someone who is not transgender.

PC Culture Has Too Great an Impact on Language

Jeremy Styron

Jeremy Styron is news editor at the News-Herald, *in Tennessee's Loudon County.*

I n this new age of safe spaces, trigger warnings, microaggressions, hypersensitivity and self-infantilization that have spread across American college campuses the last several years, school administrators and professionals—the very people who should be preparing young adults for life in a sometimes harsh and cruel world—are now targeting language itself.

The idea behind the current culture, at first, was to protect victims of abuse, rape or other violent crimes from certain words or ideas that may "trigger" recurrent thoughts or feelings that force them to relive the original incident. Thus, students could choose to opt out from having to read material they might find offensive.

Putting aside the question of whether colleges have a responsibility to shield students in this way, not only is this avoidance strategy unsupported by modern psychology—safe, controlled exposure therapy is one of the main treatments for post-traumatic stress disorder and other forms of trauma—this culture of protectionism has now outgrown its original purpose and branched out to entire campuses.

In this environment, even mentally and emotionally healthy students can say they were offended by a certain book, play or lecture, and college administrators have little, if any, way to vet their claims. Over the years, this has led to an expansion of the word "offensive," such that some of the most innocuous statements have now been labeled as a microaggressions toward some group or another.

"PC culture off the rails," by Jeremy Styron, News-Herald, August 24, 2016. Reprinted by permission.

The results of this process have been head-scratching to say the least.

"Some recent campus actions border on the surreal," Greg Lukianoff and Jonathan Haidt wrote in their important essay for The Atlantic, "The Coddling of the American Mind."

The writers pointed out one example in which an Asian American organization, hoping to bring awareness to microaggressions against other Asian students, set up a presentation that included statements such as, "Aren't you supposed to be good at math?" and "I'm colorblind! I don't see race." Much to their dismay, they experienced resistance when other Asian students claimed to be offended by the display itself, even though the effort was completely well-intentioned.

"The association removed the installation, and its president wrote an e-mail to the entire student body apologizing to anyone who was 'triggered or hurt by the content of the microaggressions,'" according to Lukianoff and Haidt.

In another case a couple years ago, sentences like, "America is the land of opportunity" and "I believe the most qualified person should get the job," were blacklisted as offensive by a group of administrators at 10 schools in the University of California college system.

Taken to its most extreme application, college students will scarce be able to read and discuss any classic work of literature for fear that it may prick their sensibilities. Think of college literature classes sans Dante's "Inferno" with its nine circles of hellish torments for the damned, or Shakespeare with his tangle of perversions and various patricides and matricides, or "Uncle Tom's Cabin" with its depiction of slavery and subjugation in the antebellum South.

"The ultimate aim, it seems, is to turn campuses into 'safe spaces' where young adults are shielded from words and ideas that make some uncomfortable," Lukianoff and Haidt wrote. "And more than the last (wave of political correctness in the 1980s and 90s), this movement seeks to punish anyone who interferes with that aim, even accidentally. You might call this impulse vindictive protectiveness. It is creating a culture in which everyone must think twice before speaking up, lest they face charges of insensitivity, aggression or worse."

Thankfully, to my knowledge, colleges haven't gone so far as to ban entire books—a true Orwellian nightmare—but some syllabi now come with "trigger warnings" alerting students that material to be studied in the class may be offensive.

"Astonishingly, some of the literary works advocates claim need warning labels for adult college students are often read by high school students, such as 'The Great Gatsby' and 'The Merchant of Venice,'" according to Atlantic contributor Karen Swallow Prior.

Prior, an English professor, recalled a student of hers who missed class time because she was offended by a discussion on Thomas Hardy's "Tess of the d'Urbervilles," which depicts the rape of the main character.

"A trigger warning might have prevented—or perhaps merely ensured—these absences," Prior wrote. "But a person traumatized by reading a Victorian novel is a person in need of help, and the entire episode brought about the small crisis, which resulted in a more important outcome: getting her connected with a college counselor."

In any case, colleges like Princeton University have now moved beyond safe spaces and trigger warnings and gone a step farther in these experiments in political correctness, encouraging the use of gender-neutral pronouns and more inclusive language. The school's human resources department recently sent out a memo to staffers suggesting that they use more generic terms when referring to different types of people in official school communications.

Guidelines include using the second person voice, like "you" and "your," rather than "his" or "her," gender neutral job titles like "actor" instead of "actress" and even nixing broad terms like "mankind" to refer to humanity.

While some guidelines like using "their" actually do make a lot of sense to avoid awkward constructions like "his or her," others like "freshman" and "forefathers" for "first-year student" and "ancestors," respectively, are, at best, unnecessarily pedantic or, at worst, asinine.

As if that weren't enough, the University of Wisconsin-Milwaukee went so far as to try to eschew the term "politically correct" altogether, branding it as its own microaggression and suggesting that students stop using it. According to the Just Words campaign, terms like "politically correct" and "PC" are "a way to deflect, (and say) that people are being too 'sensitive' and police language."

The problem, of course, is that people are, indeed, being too reactionary in some of the examples I have pointed out, and switching out a few words isn't going to destroy the patriarchy, silence the trolls or end misogyny. Only progress and the march of time can do that.

What all of this does show is an utter paralysis of language and an inability to face the world, with all its failings, as well-adjusted and reasoning adults who refuse to approach life behind the stultifying confines of muzzles and blinders.

Political Correctness Has Made Us Lose Perspective

Daphne Patai

Daphne Patai is a professor in the Department of Languages, Literatures, and Cultures at the University of Massachusetts Amherst. She is the author of, among other books, What Price Utopia? Essays on Ideological Policing, Feminism, and Academic Affairs.

How can it be that, in the face of daily news of murders, grotesque punishments, and open oppression by radicals abroad, here at home American college students, who have grown up with degrees of freedom and autonomy virtually unknown in most times and places, agitate for restrictions on their own campuses, demand rules, regulations, and censorship in the name of their versions of justice?

I don't think the answer to this question is that "this generation" of American college students is just more authoritarian in their way of thinking than their predecessors, or more impassioned about their political commitments. Nor do I think that they have been brainwashed by their families or school teachers—though this too plays a role.

What has happened is that over the past couple of decades "political correctness" became mainstreamed: it went from characterizing only certain parts of the university (above all "identity" programs, such as women's studies, openly committed to particular kinds of social change and intolerant of divergent views) to enjoying an obligatory and sincere endorsement by many faculty and administrators. This involves a massive redefinition of what higher education is and ought to be.

"How Political Correctness Corrupted the Colleges," Daphne Patai, Minding the Campus, December 13, 2015. Reprinted by permission.

All the Dread Isms

Not that this is news. In the early 1990s, when I was still in women's studies, some professors required their white students to disclose their first experience with blacks, and, if they declined to do so, the recalcitrant students were accused of being "in denial" about their own racism. Charges of racism were proving very effective in shutting down discussion and leaving even people who knew better speechless,

What has changed since is that charges of racism, sexism, and other dreaded –isms have become ever more commonplace, so that entire institutions, not just individual professors and administrators, live in fear of having such charges lobbed their way. Thus, today, it is common for universities to have orientation programs for first-year students that implicitly aim to indoctrinate them about the attitudes and words considered not just rude or thoughtless but actionable. And to have speech codes and harassment policies that all too often are in clear violation of the Constitution.

The brouhaha at the University of Missouri and at Yale, for example, perfectly illustrates the shift. What a heady feeling, to be able to push administrators and faculty into resigning, with or without official self abnegation. And with proliferating protective measures undertaken by universities (with their ever-expanding corps of administrators), is it any wonder that the supposed adults in academe become more disempowered, more fearful of being charged with one of the stigmatizing –isms?

Somehow, in America, the more students in fact enter universities, the more "flexible" our course offerings and activities, the easier it is to get a degree, the more aggrieved students feel by the persistence of complexity in their social environment. And the unsurprising result for students who know little history and less world politics is clear: what is being demanded by protesting students is a kind of control over others that would seem to have no place in a free society. But how are they to know this, if they have little knowledge and simple views of their own society and its place in the world?

The situation is not helped by the readiness with which what used to be serious intellectual venues now join in the fray. In *The New Yorker*, on Nov. 10, 2015, for example, Jelani Cobb has an article whose very title lays out the parameters of acceptable speech. It is called "Race and the Free-Speech Diversion." Such a juxtaposition both dismisses free speech and delegitimizes concerns about it at the outset.

It's hard to believe Americans would be so quick to adopt such a cavalier attitude toward one of our most valuable rights if they had actual experience of the repressive dictatorships that existed and still exist in various parts of the world. But the worst part is that these angry students and their academic abettors know and understand the First Amendment. Yet, they actively and open blatantly oppose it, believing that only the speech they approve of should be protected. The same attitudes prevail with rights of due process, routinely violated on college campuses. Why should those accused of using a racist slur or engaging in an unwanted touch or tasteless joke have any rights? Why shouldn't they at once be punished? Forced to apologize, to grovel, to resign? This is the climate of vigilantism and instant (in) justice that prevails. And it should surprise no one that students will use whatever weapons come their way.

The Oppression Sweepstakes

Way back in 1994, Noretta Koertge, a philosopher of science and I used the term "oppression sweepstakes" in our book *Professing Feminism* to describe the unseemly competition in academe (though not only there) for most oppressed status. We lamented that young women were opportunistically embracing the rhetoric of victimhood. Students were also learning to spot "sexual harassment" everywhere around them, thanks to regulations that became ever broader and looser, the better to catch any offending word, look, innuendo, or gesture. Due process, like First Amendment rights, became just another quaint notion to be despised by campus justice warriors.

I remember the first time that a student asked me (in class) to give "trigger warnings" about material I was assigning. That was perhaps ten years ago. Now that term, too, is commonplace. Since then, hypersensitivity and the search for grievances have only intensified. As big problems disappear, little ones are forced into their place, and so we get "micro-aggression," a sublime new term by which victim groups can keep complaining when the main sources of complaint have all but disappeared. Imagine the difficulty if one had to give up victimhood.

What are the implications of the fact that accusations of racism and sexism are so popular? One obvious one is that, far from being a society riddled with social injustice, the U.S. has made so much progress that such charges are cast routinely and fearlessly for they prove amazingly effective in delegitimizing others. A neat one-up move that has effortlessly worked its way into our culture.

Being called a racist automatically cripples (excuse the ableist language) the accused, since any response is immediately cast as evidence that one is simply in denial and trying to protect one's privilege. And having "privilege" has itself become a slur, another tool in the arsenal designed to impede opposing, or even just differing, points of views. Scores of dystopian fictions, films, and realities have done little to dissuade these campus rebels from a belief that their version of equality and justice can be imposed by fiat, with no serious negative consequences to themselves.

It's Who Says It, Not What's Said

Identity politics, rooted in race, gender, sexual orientation (and an ever-expanding list of other protected categories), creates a climate in which the key element is not what one says but who says it. The result: only certain people have the right to say certain things. And since identity in fact does not tell us all we need to know about a person's views, beliefs, commitments, or actions, many additional terms have been created to curtail the speech and attack the legitimacy of those with dissenting views, terms like "Uncle Tom," "Oreo," "not a real woman," or "heteronormativity." Thus, identity politics has morphed from actually requiring evidence of discrimination to merely verbalizing the claim to a supposedly oppressed identity and constantly hurt feelings.

When truth and falsity are determined by who speaks, not what is said or what relationship it bears to reality, we're in free fall, and one can expect that those who yell loudest and claim the greatest oppression will rule. Not a pretty picture, and certainly not the way a democracy is supposed to function. Bertrand Russell referred to this many years ago with his ironic phrase regarding "the superior virtue of the oppressed."

Intolerance with Moral Superiority

But this snapshot of some of the most popular gotcha games of our time does not suggest to me that students want to be treated like children, or that they genuinely want university administrators to protect them from unpleasantness and discomfort.

That is far too innocent a view of their energetic protests. Their actions suggest more worldly aims: they want to be tyrants, able to impose their will while disguising that drive with claims of moral superiority to those around them.

And a good deal of the responsibility for this state of affairs rests with faculty and administrators. Universities are not the only places attacking liberal values and the Western tradition, but what is perhaps surprising is that they're not even willing to defend themselves as places where serious learning intellectual efforts are supposed to go on. What else does their desperate commitment to so-called social justice, community activism, and all the rest of the litany amount to? Having long ago abdicated intellectual leadership in favor of feel-good phony politics and self-defeating new definitions of their missions, these agents of the university are hardly in a position to protest students' endless pursuits of these selfsame goals, which must rest on grievances and slights, real or imagined.

But, alas, when professors stop defending their academic endeavors in intellectual terms and opt instead for ersatz politics, they are rapidly outclassed by young people who can do that better: with more energy, more time, more anger. Hence, unable to compete, professors instead attempt to ingratiate ourselves with students, hoping (not very effectively, it turns out) to avoid getting caught up in their attacks.

Why, then, be surprised when students use turn against those very administrators and faculty who have been capitulating to them for years? And so students demand respect without earning it, status without achievement, and instantaneous action against the offenses they ferret out all around them.

Like other tyrants, petty or not, students engaging in phony revolutionary claims, these students just want to have their own way, impose their ideas, and be done with it. Hence they shout down speakers, get invitations rescinded, and disrupt campus activities.

They may be infantile in their yelling and screaming, but that doesn't mean they are actually seeking adult guidance. Not at all—they're trying to intimidate their elders into further subjection and are achieving marked success. And they bravely do this in the comfy atmosphere of the modern university.

Isn't it time for faculty to say: How you feel is your own affair. Feelings get hurt; that's life. People can be unpleasant, true. But what matters here is what you do. You're here to learn, to develop intellectually, and that requires effort and commitment, not moments of high drama and self-exaltation. Not every slight is an assault, every unkind word an instance of discrimination.

You want to know about inequality and pain? Just travel around the world and see what the absence of liberal values and functioning civil rights leads to, and then come back and see if continuing to complain about the horrendous inequities of your university is still your best bet for creating a better world.

Political Correctness Has Crossed the Line

Abri Brancken

Abri Brancken is founder and chairperson of the Brancken Group, and serves as the senior pastor of the Mairangi Bay Community Church in Auckland, New Zealand. He is an author, artist, and strategic life coach.

O ne of the greatest threats to the liberty and freedom of any individual, society or nation is the idea that in order to coexist and progress as a whole we need to embrace extreme political correctness. The political correctness movement has taken the world by storm, yet few people are aware of the dangers it presents. There is no doubt in my mind that in recent years the political correctness movement has gone way too far and the negative impact thereof is beginning to surface. So what is the problem with extreme political correctness?

Firstly, political correctness often hides, bends or distorts the truth in order to fit the parameters of not offending certain groups of people. For some, especially the media and political leaders, being politically correct has become the ultimate goal to achieve, regardless of how the actual truth needs to be obscured or raped in the process. The fear of being labeled a sexist, racist or being insensitive to certain people and groups outweighs personal devotion to truth and thus the allegiance of many leaders these days lies with compromise, deceit and untruthfulness. In many nations truth has become the new hate speech. The thing is this, you will not always be able to please everyone, for if you really want to, great sacrifices will need to be made which will include liberty and freedom. In order to be politically correct, many Western countries are being sacrificed on this movements' altar as it continues to push for the implementation of laws and policies that include the sacrifice of own culture, customs, traditional values and even future existence. The goal of not offending certain groups of people such as radical religious groups and unbalanced human rights organizations is undoubtedly leading towards the demise of the West. Should foreigners who choose to move to and live in Western countries (or any country for that matter) respect those countries' laws and culture? Definitely, but we all know that is not always the case. When misconduct, crime, and unacceptable religious radicalism needs to be addressed, political correctness prohibits those who want to address such issues by becoming the silencer for the voice of reason and concern. If you stand for nothing, you will fall for anything, and that is exactly what is happening to many Western countries at this moment. Fear and intimidation is one of the political correctness movement's greatest weapons and sadly it often protects the guilty instead of the innocent. Truth is hate to those that hate the truth.

Secondly, extreme political correctness breeds a culture where people lose their ability to deal with correction and constructive criticism. Correction and constructive criticism do not necessarily equal hate speech or discrimination! It is vitally important that we are able to expose and address and correct national and personal issues such as government corruption and incompetence, our cultural differences, our fears, worries, hopes, feelings and aspirations without being labeled sexist or racist. Unless we are able to honestly speak about the issues of life without fearing that others will instantly take an offence, we will never progress towards social maturity and overcome our insecurities and ignorance. A society that dooms discussion of important and relevant issues is doomed in itself. Correction is not the enemy. Resisting correction and the denial of failure is. I have come to learn that if a person is insecure about whom they are and their abilities, they become easily offended by those who disagree with or challenge them. The problem does not necessarily lie with the person presenting the challenge, but with the one being challenged. Personal insecurity and fear often hinders those being challenged from evaluating the challenge objectively and to see it as an opportunity to grow by making the necessary corrections and adjustments if needed. Sadly, many people these days would rather blame the person exposing misconduct, incompetence and corruption as being a racist or lacking nationalism instead of correcting the mistakes. If we are not allowed to voice our concerns to those whose conduct is unacceptable, those in the wrong will lose their ability to deal with correction as they will continue to believe that they are right in what they do regardless the negative impact that their actions might have on those around them.

Thirdly, political correctness has become the whip of retaliation for those who are too insecure to face the fact that they have messed up or for those who are not really interested to engage in meaningful discussion. It is easier to stigmatize and discredit the whistleblower of corruption by labeling him or her as being racist or a non-nationalist rather than taking the responsibility for personal, organizational or governmental failure and corruption. To some degree, the political correctness movement has become a safe haven for politicians and groups to hide incompetence and failure. If you take some governments on, they will label you as being a sexist or racist and thereby put the focus on you through unfair discrediting. Very often those who advocate speech that is politically correct are the first ones to be politically incorrect by falsely or wrongfully criticizing those who dare to challenge them.

The original intent of the political correctness movement may have been good, but it has crossed the line and has evolved into an insensitive monster of destruction. Needless to say, I am not advocating that we should be insensitive towards others, saying what we want, when we want, in the way we want to? Absolutely not, but neither should we refrain from addressing important issues such as corruption, incompetence and religious radicalism simply because we do not want to be labelled as a racist, sexist or insensitive. At times we need to call a "spade a spade." To "tip toe" around issues in order to be politically correct is wrong. Yes, it is good to encourage each other to be sensitive towards one another, especially when dealing with sensitive issues like race, religion, gender, physical abilities, etc., but modern day political correctness can easily and often become the barrier that actually hinders us from making real progress. In fact, I am beginning to wonder if political correctness has become nothing more than censorship in disguise. Leaders who try so hard to be politically correct often fail in providing clear direction for those whom they are supposed to lead. To always be politically correct and still make the right decisions is not always possible. There comes a time when you need to choose between keeping everyone happy or make the tough decisions and risk being labelled a whistle blower, racist or sexist in addressing issues that beckon to be addressed. Once again, am I advocating insensitivity towards others and the right to offend? No, but it is also not right to sacrifice truth for the sake of keeping everyone happy. There is a balance we need to uphold in life, and that balance demands that one cannot always stand in agreement with everyone.

For Christians, to deny common sense and to violate Biblical morals and ethics simply to be politically correct is wrong. Pastors and church leaders cannot remain silent when it comes to addressing issues such as abortion, the sanctity of marriage and Biblical truth in general. Christians are not commanded in Scripture to abandon truth and justice for the sake of making everyone feel good all the time. Christians are definitely called to be meek, but not weak and we should not confuse the two. Jesus loved people and reached out to everyone, yet in His meekness He was never weak in standing for what was right, even if it meant being ridiculed and insulted for doing so. Many Christian leaders have become passive in addressing issues that need to be addressed simply because they are afraid of the back lash that can come from those who propagate extreme political correctness. The idea that Christians should embrace a neutral view in order to appease everyone is not Biblically endorsed. We can never enjoy true unity with others if we sacrifice truth in the process. To endorse sin for the sake of unity is sin in itself.

In a society, there can be diversity within the greater unity, but it takes wisdom and maturity to manage it. The easy way out is to mold everyone in society into thinking the same, doing the same and believing the same and that is what political correctness often tries to achieve. Freedom of expression cannot survive in a nation where political correctness has become the judge and referee of how we can speak. Sometimes choosing to play the political correct card is to play the loosing card. Needless to say, with freedom of expression comes responsibility. Unless our freedom of expression is guided by Biblical morals and ethics, our expressions will quickly become the cause of unnecessary conflict and division. Our words should reflect grace, wisdom and understanding and our constructive criticism or correction should be communicated in such a way that it respects others while at the same time presenting clear direction and answers to the various complex issues we are facing today.

There Is a Connection Between Views on Political Correctness and Personal Experience

Natalia Khosla and Sean McElwee

Natalia Khosla is a researcher at Demos and Sean McElwee is a policy analyst for Demos.

I s Donald Trump really speaking for a "silent" majority of Americans when he says that political correctness is a scourge on the nation? Or do most Americans deeply value tolerance and inclusivity? The answer to this question may well decide the election this fall, so we decided to crunch the numbers. The data suggests that like so much in our changing society, your perspective depends on where you sit. And one key source of this divide is perceptions of continued discrimination in our society.

To explore views about political correctness, we used the American National Election Studies (ANES) 2016 pilot survey, a 1,200 person survey performed in January of this year.[1] ANES includes two questions that ask respondents if they think society needs to change the way it talks to be more sensitive to people from different backgrounds or if society has gone too far and people are too easily offended. There are two slightly differently worded questions on the same topic that are each asked to half of the respondents chosen at random.[2] We combined the two questions and then examined people who said society needs to be "a lot" and "a little" more sensitive, and then separately those who said society is "a lot" and "a little" too easily offended. ANES also asks respondents how much discrimination they think there is against a number of groups on a scale of 1 to 5, with blacks being one of the groups. We combined responses of "a great deal" and

"New Research Findings: People Who Say Society Is Too Politically Correct Tend Not to Have Experienced Discrimination," Natalia Khosla, Demos, June 1, 2016. Reprinted by permission.

"a lot" of discrimination, "a little" and "a moderate amount" of discrimination, and "no discrimination at all."

We find that those who believe society is becoming overly politically correct also tend to believe there is less discrimination in society against African-Americans. We also find they are less likely to say there is discrimination against gays and lesbians. The chart below shows how much discrimination respondents perceive against African-Americans based on their views on more "politically correct" or inclusive language.

Question: How Much Discrimination Is There Against African-Americans in the U.S. ?

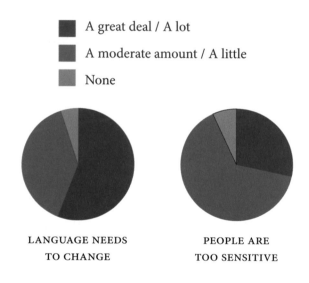

■ A great deal / A lot

■ A moderate amount / A little

■ None

LANGUAGE NEEDS
TO CHANGE

PEOPLE ARE
TOO SENSITIVE

SOURCE: McElwee and Khosla

Twenty-eight percent of respondents (and 32 percent of white respondents) say that African-Americans face "a little" or "no" discrimination despite overwhelming evidence and personal accounts of blatant discrimination on a daily basis against groups based on their race, gender, sexuality, and other identities. One study finds that "John" will be offered $4,000 more than "Jennifer" for the same job. Another finds that resumes with white-sounding names are more likely to be asked for an interview than identical resumes with black-sounding names.

Percentage of People Discriminated Against, Who Believe Language Should Be More Inclusive

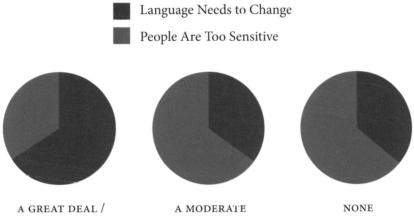

■ Language Needs to Change

■ People Are Too Sensitive

| A GREAT DEAL / A LOT | A MODERATE AMOUNT / A LITTLE | NONE |

SOURCE: McElwee and Khosla

Somewhat unsurprisingly, there are strong racial divides on the question of political correctness, with whites more likely to say that "people are too easily offended:" 71% of whites, compared to only 34% of blacks and 42% of all people of color agree with this. We also find that those who faced discrimination based on their skin color are more likely to support changing language norms, and this holds true even among only people of color (which ensures the result doesn't merely reflect racial differences in views on political correctness).

Optimistically though, these data indicate that the reverse is also true: those who recognize that there is a great deal of discrimination against blacks are more likely to believe society needs to become more sensitive. The chart below shows that whites who say that blacks face "a great deal" or "a lot" of discrimination are more likely to say language needs to change.

Percentage of White People Who Believe Language Should Change Based on Discrimination Against African-Americans

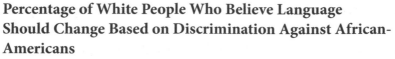

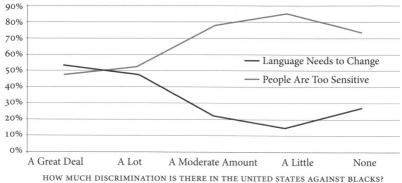

HOW MUCH DISCRIMINATION IS THERE IN THE UNITED STATES AGAINST BLACKS?

SOURCE: McElwee and Khosla

Also optimistically, whites who recognize that there is a great deal of discrimination against blacks are much more likely to believe that society needs to become more inclusive than whites who deny racial bias.

The data are clear: those who acknowledge that discrimination exists and have experienced it themselves think society needs to become more sensitive to people from different backgrounds. Those who haven't, don't. The majority of people who believe society is overly politically correct, then, are likely speaking from their own lived experience: they may not have experienced discrimination or may not think it occurs much, so when people take offense, they believe society is simply being too sensitive.

These differences of opinion are certainly important, but at some point the question of how inclusive the dominant society must be to the concerns of different people will have to move beyond the realm of personal preference. The racial and gender anxiety shuddering through this election shows that this time may have come. The United States is becoming a truly pluralistic nation, with residents and citizens who have roots in every community on the globe, and more individuals are demanding to express their gender and sexuality as they feel it. That diversity can be our greatest asset as a nation, but only if we forge a common understanding of the discrimination that exists, and a language that works for all of us.

Footnotes

1. The ANES has conducted national surveys of the American public since 1948. It is widely used by political scientists. Leading political scientists Stephen Ansolabehere and Brian Schaffner have confirmed the accuracy of opt-in panels (their study examines a survey completed by YouGov, the same firm used by the 2016 ANES pilot study). The questions on the 2016 pilot related to race were formulated by a group of scholars whose expertise is racial attitudes.

2. The full wording of the questions can be found here. The two versions of the political correctness question are:

   1. There's been a lot of talk lately about "political correctness." Some people think that the way people talk needs to change with the times to be more sensitive to people from different backgrounds. Others think that this has already gone too far and many people are just too easily offended. Which is closer to your opinion?

   2. Some people think that the way people talk needs to change with the times to be more sensitive to people from different backgrounds. Others think that this has already gone too far and many people are just too easily offended. Which is closer to your opinion?

Political Correctness Protects More Than It Harms

Aoife Kelly

Aoife Kelly has written for publications including Headstuff *and* Bust *magazine.*

Stephen Fry recently appeared on YouTube talk show *The Rubin Report*, a current events show which claims to take a "politically incorrect approach" to politics, religion and the media. I always get that mild sense of dread when I hear the words "politically incorrect." Not because I'm a spoiled millennial—although maybe I am that too—but because it's highly likely that whatever follows is going to be fairly depressing. The poster boy for "political incorrectness" these days is the ignorant, racist and misogynistic Donald Trump, so I don't automatically assume that a media outlet proudly wearing that label will be all that respectful, intelligent or balanced. If Stephen Fry's episode is anything to go by, I was not far wrong. The comedian slammed the immaturity of society, insisting that we all grow up. According to Fry, in this age of information, when young people are becoming more engaged in politics, and very little can happen in the world without reams of articles, opinion pieces and tweets discussing its nuances and implications, no one can handle complexity. No one, except of course, Mr. Stephen Fry.

This is only mildly annoying, the kind of thing you would expect from an educated older man with a superiority complex, bemoaning the perceived laziness and stupidity of the next generation. But he then went on, almost unbelievably, to berate survivors of childhood sexual abuse, admonishing them for their "self-pity" and nastily suggesting that they grow up, as nobody feels sorry for them.

"Political Correctness Is Not Harming Our Society, Despite What Stephen Fry Might Think," by Aoife Kelly, Headstuff.org, April 15, 2016. Reprinted by permission.

This current strain of anti-PC activism seems to be stronger than any previous manifestations. If it's taking down well-respected and admired celebrities like Stephen Fry, we should be worried. Fry's comments were absolutely appalling, and totally unwarranted. The nastiness, the lack of compassion, the visible disgust with which he said it; what could have prompted this vitriol on a widely-viewed talk show?

Perhaps he felt safe in the knowledge that he was surrounded by his anti-PC family, all similarly middle-class white men with chips on their shoulders, lamenting the bygone days when you could demean women or spout racial abuse with no repercussions; a judgement-free community of political incorrectness. A safe space, if you will.

Now, don't get me wrong. I've read *1984* too. I, too, worry that the thought police might be coming for us all, to plunge us into some dull Orwellian nightmare-realm of censorship. A world where we are told what to think, what to believe, what to wear, what to do with our bodies. As a woman living in a patriarchal society, surrounded by a sexist media and waiting on a government to decide if I should have reproductive rights, I certainly can't imagine what a world like that would be like!

Leaving aside the abhorrent ugliness and cruelty in Fry's comments, the heart of the problem is that he doesn't seem to know who he is addressing. Sure, we've all heard that the coddled millennials and Tumblr-feminists are logging into our Facebooks in the night to steal our free speech. And maybe it's the spectre of this imaginary army of cry-babies that Fry and his ilk think they're defending themselves against.

But in reality, his callous comments are not going to whip some "overly-sensitive teenagers" or "regressive liberals" (as *The Rubin Report* refers to them) into shape, and get them to toughen up like they had to "back in my day." In reality, he is insulting the real human beings suffering from PTSD or living in the shadow of a traumatic experience, real sufferers of depression, anxiety or other mental illnesses for whom Fry himself has been such an influential spokesperson.

People like Stephen Fry have taken serious issue with the introduction of trigger warnings and safe spaces in college campuses and online. Personally, I don't see the harm. Though they may not go by that name, trigger warnings are already everywhere. You'll find them on DVDs, on CDs, and a presenter will introduce *Skins* on Channel 4 with the words "Strong language from the start."

This isn't an exclusionary tactic, and it isn't censorship. It's actually even more inclusive—a trigger warning lets you know what's in store, and trusts that with that knowledge you can make a decision on your own: Do I want to read this? Do I want to watch this? I imagine there are more than a few survivors of sexual assault who would have liked to have had that choice before listening to Fry's heartless rant.

As the wonderful feminist author Roxane Gay writes in her powerful personal essay "The Safety of Illusion/The Illusion of Safety," "trigger warnings aren't meant for those of us who don't believe in them just like the Bible wasn't written for atheists." Stephen Fry takes issue with both of these things—perhaps he believes that all things that don't apply to or benefit him personally must be abolished?

Fry complains about the "infantilism of our culture" but marches off Twitter in a strop when there's any pushback against his ideas. It's surprising that such a self-proclaimed intelligent man doesn't see the irony in this. As for political correctness, I'd like to come back to a quote by Neil Gaiman, in which he imagines "a world in which we replaced the phrase 'politically correct' wherever we could with 'treating other people with respect.'"

Stephen Fry may feel that political correctness is harming society, but his opinion is irrelevant. Safe spaces and trigger warnings are put in place for the people that need them, not for men who can exercise their free speech by insulting vulnerable people on a YouTube chat show. I would expect him, of all people, to be able to handle the complexity of that.

Organizations to Contact

The editors have compiled the following list of organizations concerned with the issues debated in this book. The descriptions are derived from materials provided by the organizations. All have publications or information available for interested readers. This list was compiled on the date of publication of the present volume; the information provided here may change. Be aware that many organizations take several weeks or longer to respond to inquiries, so allow as much time as possible.

American Association for Access, Equity, and Diversity
1701 Pennsylvania Avenue NW, Suite 206
Washington, DC 20006
(202) 349-9855
email: info@aaaed.org
website: http://www.aaaed.org

This organization began in 1794 as the American Association for Affirmative Action. The AAAED provides its members with professional training and helps them to be more successful and productive in their careers. The organization promotes understanding and advocacy of affirmative action and other equal opportunity and related compliance laws to enhance the tenets of access, inclusion, and equality in employment, economic, and educational opportunities.

American Booksellers for Free Expression
333 Westchester Avenue
White Plains, NY 10604
(800) 637-0037
email: info@bookweb.org
website: http://www.bookweb.org

American Booksellers for Free Expression's mission is to promote and protect the free exchange of ideas, particularly those contained in books, by opposing restrictions on freedom of speech. The organization issues statements on significant free expression controversies and participates in legal cases involving First Amendment rights. ABFE collaborates with like-minded groups and strives to educate book sellers, and others in the book industry, about the importance of free expression.

American Civil Liberties Union
125 Broad Street, 18th Floor
New York, NY 10004
(212) 549-2500
email: infoaclu@aclu.org
website: http://www.aclu.org

The American Civil Liberties Union defines its mission as realizing the promise of the Bill of Rights for all and expanding the reach of its guarantees to new areas. The organization was founded following the Palmer Raids of 1919-1920 and has since grown to include well over one million members. The ACLU is nonprofit and nonpartisan.

Bill of Rights Defense Committee and Defending Dissent Foundation
1100 G Street NW, Suite 500
Washington, DC 20005
(202) 529-4225
email: info@bordc.org
website: http://www.bordc.org

This organization strives to protect the right of expression, with the goal of strengthening participatory democracy. The BORDC works to ensure government accountability and transparency. Its goals also include ending profiling based on personal characteristics.

Leadership Conference on Civil Rights

1620 L Street NW, Suite 1100
Washington, DC 20036
(202) 466-3311
website: http://www.civilrights.org

This coalition includes more than 200 national organizations, all of which strive to promote and protect the civil and human rights of all persons in the US. The Leadership Conference engages in legislative advocacy with the goal of creating a more open and just society. Its education and research arm is the Education Fund.

National Coalition Against Censorship

19 Fulton Street, Suite 407
New York, NY 10038
(212) 807-6222
email: ncac@ncac.org
website: http://www.ncac.org

The National Coalition Against Censorship's mission is to promote freedom of thought, inquiry, and expression and oppose censorship in all its forms. The organization formed in response to the 1973 Supreme Court decision in *Miller v. California*. The NCAC includes an alliance of more than fifty national nonprofit organizations and engages in direct advocacy and education to support First Amendment principles.

National Freedom of Information Coalition

Missouri School of Journalism
101E Reynolds Journalism Institute
Columbia, MO 65211
(573) 882-4856
email: nfoic@nfoic.org
website: http://www.nfoic.org

This organization works to protect people's right to open government. Its goal is to ensure that state and local governments and public institutions have laws, policies, and procedures to facilitate the public's access to their records and proceedings. This nonpartisan organization is an alliance of state and regional affiliates that share its goals.

National Urban League
120 Wall Street
New York, NY 10005
(212) 558-5300
website: http://nul.iamempowered.com
The National Urban League is a historic civil rights organization dedicated to economic empowerment in order to elevate the standard of living in historically underserved urban communities. This national organization spearheads the efforts of its local affiliates through the development of programs, public policy research, and advocacy. The direct services this organization provides impact and improve the lives of more than two million people in the US.

People for the American Way
1101 15th Street NW, Suite 600
Washington, DC 20005
(202) 467-4999
email: pfaw@pfaw.org
website: http://www.pfaw.org

This organization was founded in 1981 by television and film producer Norman Lear and the late congresswoman Barbara Jordan. People for the American Way and the People for the American Way Foundation are progressive advocacy organizations founded to fight right-wing extremism and defend constitutional values under attack. This includes free expression, religious liberty, equal justice under the law, and the right to meaningfully participate in our democracy.

Race Forward: The Center for Racial Justice
Innovation
32 Broadway, Suite 1801
New York, NY 10004
(212) 513-1367
email: media@raceforward.org
website: http://www.raceforward.org

Founded in 1981, Race Forward advances racial justice through research, media, and practice. This organization's mission is to build awareness, solutions, and leadership for racial justice by generating transformative ideas, information, and experiences. Race Forward envisions a vibrant world in which people of all races create, share, and enjoy resources and relationships equitably, unleashing individual potential, embracing collective responsibility, and generating global prosperity.

Reporters Committee for Freedom of the Press
1156 15th Street NW, Suite 1250
Washington, DC 20005
(800) 336-4243
email: info@rcfp.org
website: http://www.rcfp.org

This organization provides free legal resources, support, and advocacy to protect the First Amendment and freedom of information rights of journalists working in areas where US law applies, regardless of the medium in which their work appears. This organization is funded by corporate, foundation, and individual contributions. Available services include a Legal Defense Hotline, Amicus Briefs and Statements of Support, and publications and resources on a range of relevant topics.

Bibliography

Books

ACLU. *The Constitution of the United States of America.* Pocket ed. New York, NY: ACLU, 2007.

Nick Adams. *Retaking America: Crushing Political Correctness.* New York, NY: Post Hill Press, 2016.

Dave Anderson. *If You Don't Make Waves, You'll Drown.* Hoboken, NJ: John Wiley & Sons, 2013.

Timothy Garton Ash. *Free Speech: Ten Principles for a Connected World.* New Haven, CT, and London, UK: Yale University Press, 2016.

John Calvert. *If You Don't Mind My Saying So.* Bloomington, IN: Xlibris Corporation, 2016.

John C. Domino. *Civil Rights and Liberties in the 21st Century.* New York, NY: Routledge, 2018.

Jim Dueck. *How Political Correctness Weakens Schools.* Lanham, MD: Rowman & Littlefield Publishers Inc., 2016.

Thomas Gibbons. *Free Speech in the New Media.* New York, NY: Routledge, 2016.

Kirsten Powers. *The Silencing: How the Left Is Killing Free Speech.* Washington, DC: Regnery Publishing, 2015.

Howard Schwartz. *Political Correctness and the Destruction of Social Order: Chronicling the Rise of the Pristine Self.* New York, NY: Springer International Publishing, 2016.

Kara E. Stooksbury, John M. Scheb II, Otis H. Stephens Jr., eds. *Encyclopedia of American Civil Rights and Liberties (4 Volumes): Revised and Expanded Edition.* 2nd ed. Santa Barbara, CA: ABC-CLIO Incorporated, 2017.

Periodicals and Internet Sources

Elizabeth Bartusiak and Syeda Sameeha, "Has Our Society Become Too Politically Correct?" The Mash, March 8, 2016. http://www.themash.com.

Jean Card, "Political Correctness Is Too Painless," *U.S. News & World Report*, May 19, 2016. http://www.usnews.com.

Jonathan Chait, "Not a Very P.C. Thing to Say," *New York Magazine*, January 27, 2015. http://www.nymag.com.

Matt Connolly and Ian Gordon, "Timeline: A Century of Racist Sports Team Names," *Mother Jones*, November 1, 2013. http://www.motherjones.com.

Debate.org, "Is Political Correctness a Good Thing?" 2017. www.debate.org.

Hannah Fingerhut, "In Political Correctness Debate, Most Americans Think Too Many People Are Easily Offended," Pew Research, July 20, 2016. http://www.pewinternet.org.

Greg Lukianoff and Jonathan Haidt, "The Coddling of the American Mind," *Atlantic*, September 2015. http://www.theatlantic.com.

Sean McElwee and Jason McDaniel, "Language Matters: Concerns About Political Correctness Are Deeply Intertwined with Race," Alternet, July 3, 2016. http://www.alternet.org.

Parker Molloy, "What Political Correctness Does and Doesn't Mean," Upworthy, December 16, 2015. http://www.upworthy.com.

Dave Schilling, "Has Politically Correct Culture Gone Too Far?" *Guardian*, December 14, 2015. http://www.theguardian.com.

Anna Silman, "'That's Not Racist, You Idiot:' Jay Leno Slams Kids for Being Too Politically Correct," Salon, March 20, 2015. http://www.salon.com.

Index